The Moscow Scene

GEOFFREY BOCCA

The Moscow Scene

STEIN AND DAY/*Publishers*/New York

First published in 1976
Copyright © 1976 by Geoffrey Bocca
All rights reserved
Designed by Ed Kaplin
Printed in the United States of America
Stein and Day/*Publishers*/Scarborough House,
Briarcliff Manor, N.Y. 10510

Library of Congress Cataloging in Publication Data

Bocca, Geoffrey.
    The Moscow scene.

    Includes index.
    1. Moscow—Description.   I. Title.
DK601.2.B6   914.7'31   75-34244
ISBN 0-8128-1912-8

Moscow: those syllables can start
A tumult in the Russian heart.
                    —Pushkin

Contents

Preface to Arrival

Getting There Is Half the Fun, They Say

I once spent three days getting to Moscow. We were snowed in at Geneva. Eventually thawed out, we headed for Zürich, which signaled us that we could not land because of a snowstorm, so we went to Frankfurt, spent a couple of days there and returned to Geneva. Ultimately we landed at Moscow Airport. It was the only time I have ever arrived in Moscow in a bad temper, which lasted about fifteen minutes. A driver was assigned to take me into town. I observed on the way that, although it was bitterly cold, there did not seem to be much snow.

The driver replied solemnly, "I think God feels He has completed his snow norm for the winter."

I was immediately in good humor again and settled down in Moscow for yet another pleasant stay.

My most recent journey was the most memorable, combining both the most comfortable and the most uncomfortable of all. The journey started in Montreal, Canada, aboard the *Stefan Batory*, the charming Polish liner, and went via Southampton and Rotterdam to Gdynia. Somehow in my years of traveling through Eastern Europe I'd missed Poland, so I planned to take the train from Gdynia to Warsaw, spend four days there, and then to Moscow.

Now when travel people in New York, or London, or Paris

say, "There are no hotel rooms (Motor Show, convention, Ideal Home Exhibition, you know)," what it means is that one may have to make a dozen or so telephone calls before one finds something. Seeking the St. Regis, one may have to settle at the Alden up on Central Park West and Eighty-fourth Street; hoping for the Savoy, one may finish up in Earl's Court. But there is always *something*.

Not so in Eastern Europe. When they say "No rooms," they mean no rooms period. In Prague I have seen Cedok, the official travel agency, close its hotel section in the middle of the working day on scores of dismayed travelers without reservations. There is nothing for it but to return to the airport and fly out *anywhere*. I have seen despairing travelers milling around in Budapest Airport and Schönefeld Airport in East Berlin who had no wish to be there at all.

The reader would presume that I, with such experiences behind me, would not be such a jackass as to make my first trip to Warsaw without a hotel reservation, but I was, and I did.

It was off season, and I had seen Communist countries empty as well as crammed, so why bother? My intention was to stroll through the fabulous Hanseatic city of Gdańsk, formerly Danzig, then get a first-class train ticket to Warsaw, enjoy a good meal, and educate myself about the Polish countryside.

In Gdańsk I called on Orbis, the official Polish travel agency, and asked them to Telex the Hotel Europaisky in Warsaw for a room and bath. I then heard the chill words, "There are no hotel rooms in Warsaw. Warsaw has been fully booked for the past six weeks. It is at the present time holding an Industrial Achievement Exhibition."

I tried to conceal my terror behind a mask of aplomb. "In that case, I will spend tonight in Gdańsk. Perhaps you can get me something in Warsaw tomorrow. I must be in Moscow in four days."

"There are no rooms in Gdańsk."

This, as *Forever Amber* would put it, was a pretty fetch. I had absolutely no room for maneuver. My visas, both Polish and Russian, were absolutely specific about arrival and departure. There was no going back, and obviously there was no standing still. I decided that if I couldn't get a hotel room in Gdańsk and I couldn't get a hotel room in Warsaw, I would rather not have a hotel room in Warsaw. I would cross that Vistula when I came to it. At least I would be rested and fed and have experienced the Polish landscape, its rivers, mountains, farms, cities.

The train steamed into Gdańsk Station, and a solid mass of humanity surged aboard. One would have thought all Poland was fleeing the Soviet Army. I assumed, amiably, that they were all in second class and my first-class ticket would be a talisman for comfort. Instead, I wedged myself, my suitcase, my attaché case and my typewriter in the corridor of a first-class carriage and contemplated (a) the next six hours as a human sardine, and (b) the arrival—at night—in a Warsaw without hotel rooms. The train moved out, belching soot. Point (c), I was going to arrive in Warsaw *very* dirty.

Within the human spirit, however, there is always *some* reserve for initiative. In my attaché case I possessed a few improving paperbacks and, more importantly, an almost full bottle of Pernod. The latter held the means of anesthesia against the hours to come, the elbows in my ribs and the heels on my feet.

But *pastis* is something that cannot, under any circumstances, be drunk straight. I needed water and a glass.

I learned that the buffet car was two coaches along, but in order to get there, I would have to be passed over the heads of two coach corridors of compressed, baggage-garnished living matter. What to do? Brain cells whirred and came up with the answer. Nothing.

And then, after half an hour, the train stopped with a sigh of brakes in open countryside. I barreled to the door, opened it and leaped onto the tracks. Ignoring yells and whistles, I sprinted up and boarded the buffet car. Opening the door almost re-

produced the ship's cabin scene in *A Night at the Opera*. East
Europeans, even the often bloody-minded Poles, tend to yield
priority to the easily recognized Western traveler, so I squeezed
without remonstrance to the buffet counter. The buffet itself was
about twice the size of an American maid's room, the kitchen
the size of a clothes closet. To a sweating steward, passing
sausage, sauerkraut and bottles of beer over rows of heads, I
said, "Water. *de l' Eau. Aqua. Agua. Wasser. Voda.*"

He spoke no English, French, Italian, Spanish, German or
Russian. A purée of more enlightened Poles, cracking my rib
cage against the counter, translated in friendly yells. The
steward said, "Pepsi, Fanta, limonade," none of which, even *in
extremis,* mixes with Pernod. "He say no water," said a Pole three
feet and four people away. I forced a hand free to point to a
boiling kettle. "That must be water, unless he's mulling vodka."

More yells. The steward reluctantly produced a couple of
bottles of water. The Poles cheered.

"Now a glass," I said.

The steward ad-libbed. My friend said apologetically. "He
say no more glasses except for Pepsi, Fanta and limonade."

I reached past the scalawag to a shelf and took a glass.
Victory! I also bought a couple of beers for insurance. The
question now was, how the mischief was I to get back to my
bags and my Pernod?

I then noticed that the train had not moved since my earlier
desperate dash. Again I got to the door, this time with arms
folded over two bottles of water, two bottles of beer and a glass.
Again I descended and ran. Being released from the pressure of
people felt like having a plaster cast removed from one's ribs.
Had the train moved, heaven knows what I would have done in
the depths of Poland.

I made it, turned my suitcase on end and assembled my bar.
I poured out a slug of the *pastis*, filling the corridor with the odor
of aniseed, and clouded it with blessed water. I also extracted an
Ed McBain Eighty-ninth Precinct paperback.

Despite the lunacy of the scene, my fellow passengers

avoided staring at me and concentrated with seeming desperation on their crosswords. They pretended I wasn't there, perhaps because my breath hung over me like an anise-flavored cloud.

The reader will now want to be informed about the Polish countryside.

It's flat. Flatter than the Polish countryside there isn't. The wonder is not that the German Panzers swept over it so fast in September 1939, but what on earth were they dawdling for? They should have done it by late afternoon, even pausing for luncheon. I looked at it for quite a while, and then turned to my Ed McBain.

Six hours later the Pernod was much reduced. I felt no pain except in my thighs, insteps, ribs and, probably, my liver. I elected to rest, sat on my suitcase and broke it, spilling my clothes on the grimy floor. My fingernails and hands had broken through the tolerance platform of filth. I struggled to the lavatory, as noisome as train lavatories always are. To my delight there remained a postage-stamp sliver of red soap. It was dry—like the faucet. I struggled back.

In due course came Warsaw Station and, beyond, the lights of Stalin's monstrous Palace of Culture. Night had fallen. Rain was also falling, in a steady downpour. My clothes were falling out of my suitcase, and there was also my attaché case and typewriter. I could think of only two things: the dream of a hot bath, and the fact that there were no rooms in Warsaw.

There were also no taxis. I took my place in a queue about half a kilometer long. In the course of the next fifteen minutes, exactly one taxi appeared with its "unoccupied" light on. Several, however, passed slowly with their lights out, and people broke rank to talk to the drivers.

Twelve days at sea in the *Stefan Batory*, and six hours by rail, had taught me something about the Poles. For one thing, when a Polish train steward says he has only Pepsi, Fanta and limonade, he also has water. I had also learned that a zloty is Polish money and not a little Dutch whore.

I broke the line, pushing an elderly lady to the ground. The driver was making a deal with a young woman with a baby in her arms. She had evidently carried it the entire trip. The hell with it; they had homes to go to, and I was homeless. "Hotel Europaisky, *prozhe*."

The taxi shook with peals of derisive laughter. This was an ambitious driver with his eyes on distant vistas, not a ridiculous five or six blocks for a sodden foreigner. A 100 zloty bill (worth $2.50, $3.50 or $5, depending on how one goes about it) fluttered onto the driver's lap. "Hop in (or something)," he said. I bundled my chaos into the taxi and we set off, past about four hundred wet and resigned Poles.

Ten minutes later I entered the majestic, crowded vestibule and approached the night room clerk with what nonchalance I could muster, hoping my face was not in the same condition as my fingernails. Hopeless—especially as my appearance was compounded by the condition of my baggage. Room clerks can spot a gentleman the moment he enters the swing doors, and it was too obvious that I wasn't one. A denizen of the Bowery or Appalachia had hopped off a freight car into the best and fullest hotel in Poland.

"A room with a bath, please," I said, smiling as brilliantly as Al Jolson singing "Mammy."

"We are completely booked for the next six weeks. There is a Polish Industrial Achievement Exhibition—"

"Surely *that* can't take long. . ."

"—followed immediately by a convention of farm managers." He said it with all the compassion of a croupier raking in one's losings.

"Then perhaps you could ring other hotels for me."

"There are only four, and they are all fully booked. I shall try the Bristol for you, but it is useless." He talked to his colleague with an expression of deepening impassivity. He put down the telephone with deliberation, like a doctor about to announce a terminal disease. "The Bristol is fully booked until the end of November. I assure you, sir, that there is not a single hotel room in Warsaw."

No rooms in Warsaw. But, by cracky, there is bottled water in a train which stocks only Pepsi, Fanta and limonade, and a taxi moves on the fuel of a hundred-zloty bill. Early memories came back to me. I had at one time, in my youth, been a room clerk myself at the Hampshire House Hotel on Central Park South in New York, with a team of colleagues as corrupt and treacherous as any described in *Hotel Splendido* by Ludwig Bemmelmans. The corner of a green ten-dollar bill winked at him from my billfold.

"Porter," the room clerk said, "take the gentleman to room 304."

I have stayed at the George V in Paris. I have stayed at the Royal Hawaiian in Waikiki Beach, the Raffles in Singapore, the Dan in Tel Aviv, the Negresco in Nice, the Excelsior in Rome, the Palace in Lausanne. Reader, no hotel room on the globe looked more beautiful than room 304 at the Europaisky in Warsaw. Love came in by the door . . . . The sweetest sight I ever saw . . . . Seventh heaven on the old third floor.

I was home dry, not intending to be for long. I flung richesse at the porter, spun the faucets in the bathroom with soot-black hands. The hot-water tap gushed brown rust for a full ten seconds. The room had not been occupied for days. Or weeks.

There followed four fascinating days in Warsaw, including perhaps the only punch-up of my adult life—with a drunken Fellow of Warsaw University, who then fell off a high stool in a wine bar in the Old Town, and was asked to leave. The Old Town, reconstructed brick by brick from the ashes of the war, is one of the most inspiring architectural achievements since the Renaissance. The fact that it is new and *not* medieval, and thus carries a whiff of Disneyland to the outside visitor, is properly unworthy. The knowledge that the city fathers, wandering among the ruins, themselves half starving and under the boot of Stalin, with no money in the national exchequer, agreed to rebuild the beautiful city exactly as it had been, is awe-inspiring. And every church was packed to the doors.

After four days I strapped up the wrecked suitcase (I had no intention of paying Mark Cross prices for a piece of shoddy plastic: if I could make it to Moscow, and *then* make it to London, I could become a civilized traveler again with the help of Simpson's of Piccadilly). I prepared to board the British Airways flight to Moscow. The heart began to beat again as it always did. Surely I could not enjoy myself as much as I had always done before. I had merely been lucky on earlier trips. Every correspondent has his lucky cities and his unlucky cities. Robert Ruark used to say that his heart leaped every time he had to go to London and sank every time he had to go to Paris. I had always been lucky in Moscow, but you can't win 'em all. Would it last?

Anyway, Moscow, here I come.

1

Moscow Pastiche

Most visitors to Moscow come back mad or frustrated. They find the city a crushing concatenation of faceless, shabby, shoving, rude and, above all, indifferent, uninterested people, pouring into the Metros in hordes that make the New York subway at rush hour seem like a stroll through cloisters. (In fact, the Moscow Metro, with fewer than half the miles of the New York subway and about one third the number of stations, carries 5 million people a day against 3 million in New York. Fewer Metro riders, however, get mugged. The mugger has not got the room to get out his switchblade.)

Even when the authorities try to do right by visitors—which is not often—they do it wrong. Today a visa to the Soviet Union is only a formality, a matter of hours. One receives a small document with two parts. One half is torn off and retained by Immigration on arrival. The other is handed over on departure. Nothing is stamped into one's passport.

The catch is that the returning visitor has absolutely nothing to show to prove he had ever visited one of the world's most mysterious lands. Neighbors can look askance at the visitor's claims of ever having been there at all. Fur hats, after all, can be bought in any department store, and the bottom carbon of his airline ticket is probably illegible. The visa on the passport used to be one of the most treasured souvenirs a visitor brought back, covered in red stars like a May Day parade in Red Square, borne with pride, like wounds sustained upon St. Crispin's Day.

Visitors to Moscow often feel they must be missing something. Or that they must be doing something wrong to be enjoying it so little. So let me say at once that they are not alone in that feeling. Businessmen, airline representatives, diplomats and foreign correspondents resident in Moscow get the same feeling of helplessness and claustrophobia. Many of the Western correspondents live in a privileged ghetto on the Sadova Samotechnaya, a broad, Stalin-built ring avenue. Almost symbolically they refer to the street as "Sad Sam."

And Moscow carries a certain eerie smell. I first noticed the smell just after the war, not in Moscow, but in the blitzed ruins of Belgrade, Yugoslavia. It was oppressive, acrid. It seemed to compound halitosis, body odor, cheap suits in need of dry cleaning, and unburied cadavers. I then smelled the same smell throughout Eastern Europe: in Budapest, Prague, Sofia. Others have commented on it. It becomes identified in the minds of all travelers with the smell of Communism itself. It follows the Red Flag like the K.G.B.

Havana smelled all right until Castro took over. Indeed, under Battista, Havana's Prado smelled like the bottom of a whore's handbag. The moment Castro opened his mouth to declare he was a Communist, the same foul wind blew over Cuba. The smell divides East and West Berlin as precisely as the Wall itself. It is, of course, the greasy smell of Soviet deisel oil. It fills the Moscow air and identifies with Moscow as perfume does with Paris and fog used to do with London, before the city cleaned itself up.

Whatever the individual reader's view is concerning President Ford and his attitude toward New York City, the aspect that hit me the hardest was that New York's financial crisis coincided with Ford's grain deal with the Soviet Union and his attempts to import Soviet oil. He actually wanted to import the Moscow pong to American cities. Not content with letting New York go down the drain, he was negotiating to bring the drain up to the noses of New York.

This, then, is patently not a travel book, though one hopes it will prove useful for the prospective traveler (and perhaps informative to the traveler who has been there and didn't like it). One of its aims is to try to show some of the humanity that illuminates, however feebly, the present-day Moscow scene and continues to survive behind the apparently impenetrable Moscow façade.

After a time Moscow oppresses everybody. The foreign correspondents, no matter how much they enjoy their assignment, no matter how well they master the language and adjust to the Moscow pattern of living, all get the overwhelming urge to escape from the place, if only for a time—to fly to London or Paris for a touch of elegance, a wisecrack from a London bus clippie, a smiling face in the street, or simply to go into a shop, buy something and come out with it neatly wrapped. All these little niceties do not exist in Moscow. Then, after a few deep breaths of freedom, a few movies in one's own language, a coffee in a sidewalk café, they are ready for their Moscow bureau again—the old frustrations and excitements of the job.

They enjoy Moscow in spite of itself. They like it in odd ways, rather like a prisoner in solitary confinement getting his kicks by racing cockroaches. They cannot forever impose themselves on each other's company. So as a favorite game, *faute de mieux*, old Moscow hands indulge in people-watching. Moscow in its own way houses as many kooks as New York or London, and one can have much innocent fun seeking them out, the way bird watchers trail birds.

In Gorky Park I saw a well-dressed young man sitting on a crowded bench. He looked contented enough as he chain-smoked. What set him apart from the other loungers was that he was sitting on the park-bench *backward*; he rested his arms on the back rest, and his chin on his arms. As the cigarette reached the end, he threw his head back, puffed out the stub in a wide arc through the air and lit another. Nobody seemed to find the sight unusual. I watched him for a good half hour and found the experience rewarding.

Russians are avid readers of books, and a resident Westerner who has seen a good "reader" will telephone his friends about it. Muscovites read books in food stores as they inch along the queues. In the Metro at rush hour, crammed together until the ribs crack, books are read held aloft like periscopes on submarines. Young couples sit in the park, hold books over each other's shoulders, and read between kisses (the kisses come as they are turning the pages). In the underpass under Manezhnaya Square I saw a reeling drunk, leaning unsteadily against a pillar, reading a book. I caught the author's name: Zane Grey.

Friday is a splendid day for people-watching. Friday is the day when young couples get married. The grim marriages of Stalin's time are no more. In those days the couple went to a registrar's office, signed a book and received a marriage receipt. That was that.

An elderly friend of mine, now in New York, was married in Moscow in the thirties, and recalls being deafened by the sobs of a woman at the next desk, reporting the death of her father. She found the occasion rather unfestive.

Nowadays Russian girls marry in white, in ankle-length dresses and white shoes. The boys wear dark suits and whatever frills they can find, like a choirboy's collar or flounced cuffs. The shoes, however, tend to be mustard brown. After the ceremony they lay a wreath on the tomb of the Unknown Soldier and then have a riotous lunch in a restaurant with a lot of vodka and very loud music.

For a touring bachelor, nothing is easier than to acquire a girl friend for the length of his stay. The Intourist hotels all have desks where theater tickets can be bought for hard currency. The bachelor, instead of buying one, buys two. Outside the Bolshoi or the Stanislavsky, before any performance, crowds of Muscovites stand, asking to buy spare tickets. Most of them are young (this is one of the many scenes which make one detest the régime and feel compassion for the people; these are educated and culture-hungry people; they cannot get tickets, while the same tickets are available to yobbos from Liverpool, Toronto and Cleveland who don't know the difference between *Giselle* and *Puss in Boots).* The bachelor offers his spare ticket to the prettiest girl he sees. She will reach into her handbag to pay. He waves the offer away, and she is his for the duration.

Even when one speaks no Russian at all there is no great problem watching an opera, or even a play, provided one knows the opera or play one is going to see. All confirmed theatergoers know *The Cherry Orchard, Three Sisters,* and *The Seagull,* and they can laugh and cry at all the right moments. Not to mention *Hamlet, Macbeth* and *The Importance of Being Earnest.* As for *Eugene Onegin* and *Prince Igor,* they go, if you will pardon the expression, without saying.

But non-Russian operas, like *Rigoletto* and *Carmen* lose considerably in translation. And Moscow divas tend, disconcertingly, to make Joan Sutherland look like Twiggy. In my most recent exposure to *Carmen* at the Bolshoi, the singer who played Don José was a dead ringer for Liberace, or even, for older readers, the wrestler Gorgeous George, with his hair dyed black instead of blond.

The Soviet tourist organization runs a chain of shops for foreigners called Berioska, meaning birch tree, the symbol (along with the knout) of Russia. Purchases are made in Western currency only. The girls in the Berioska shops are sometimes quite pleasant, occasionally even charming, perhaps because, alone among the service employees of the Soviet Union, they handle beautiful merchandise.

An achievement of which I shall always be proud was, while once staying at the National Hotel, to get all three girls in the hotel's Berioska shop absolutely plastered. For some apparently plausible reason, I succeeded in prevailing on them to lead me downstairs to the basement stockroom for a farewell party. We took down a great deal of export vodka, caviar and Soviet champagne. The girls took turns minding the shop, while the other two regaled me with some very funny jokes about Soviet officialdom.

As soon as they started falling and floundering among the cardboard cartons I knew that the party was a success. Every fifteen minutes or so one would reel up to relieve the girl on duty and be immediately replaced.

It is a fact of Russian life that no Russian can accept a gift without giving something in return, no matter how little. The three tipsy salesladies now owned lipsticks and magazines. They gave me a fat, illustrated Berioska catalogue, the nearest thing the Soviet Union possesses to a Sears, Roebuck catalogue. Each girl then solemnly autographed it.

After about an hour and a half a stern manageress descended and saw us sitting among the package cases, glasses in hand, surrounded by empty bottles. Almost word for word she repeated to me Oliver Cromwell's admonition to the rump Parliament. Apparently upstairs all hell was breaking loose, and the girls were doing their sums wrong. Nice girls.

None of them was there the next time I went to Moscow, and their successors were made of sterner stuff. In fact, nobody is *ever* there when I return to Moscow. The correspondents have changed. The Russian friends one has met have disappeared.

The chauffeurs of high government officials can now be seen wearing smart uniforms and caps. Twenty years ago even Khrushchev's chauffeur probably wore a lumberjack shirt and baggy trousers. The new spruceness provides an amusing parallel with the West. In Fleet Street, London, the chauffeurs of the newspaper editors went on strike for the right *not* to have to wear a cap. Chauffeur-driven cars—the windows curtained to protect the bureaucrats from the gaze of the masses—are far more conspicuous in Moscow than in any city in the West. They serve many purposes, for bureaucrat and chauffeur alike. The chauffeur not only picks up the bureaucrat and drives him to and from work, he also runs his personal errands to the shops and even takes his children from and to school. The chauffeur himself moonlights as a taxi driver, waiting outside the hotels in his huge black Chaika. It is not impossible that a tourist may be picked up after nightfall by the driver of Gromyko or Podgorny.

When I was last in Moscow the bureaucrats were complaining with great bitterness at a government decree thinning out the number of officials entitled to a chauffeur-driven car. This has always been their most valued perquisite. Many have never sat behind the wheel in their lives, and the government was proposing to give them driving lessons.

Despite their heavy reading few Muscovites seem to need spectacles, but nearly all seem to chain-smoke to a terrifying degree. Cigarette packs do not carry health warnings. So the world crisis may end when our principal adversary collapses of endemic lung cancer.

In 1973 Moscow issued its first telephone directory since 1958. Only fifty thousand copies were printed; it cost twelve rubles, or sixteen dollars, and sold on a first-come, first-served basis. The directory omits names of all Western businessmen, diplomats, airlines and news bureaus, presumably in case Muscovites might be tempted to ring them up to say what a lousy country they live in. The four-volume edition lists 700,000 names. The single-volume Manhattan telephone directory lists a million names, and the four-volume London directory, 3 million names. The Moscow directory is not available in any public place.

Winter, not summer, is the season to see Moscow. For one thing, it is not so submerged in other tourists and, for another, Moscow under the snow is one of the world's most magical cities. Muscovites have neither the clothes nor the living space for two separate wardrobes, so the winter wardrobe must take priority. In the summer girls wear dowdy dresses and sandals, the men open-necked shirts, nondescript trousers and sandals. The effect is not esthetic.

But in winter Muscovites are magnificent in their boots, mitts and overcoats. Most wear leather hats with earflaps.

Fur hats are usually reserved for high officials or for the K.G.B. By this ludicrous system officials who are supposed to be anonymous, like the secret police, stick out like whitlows. The ordinary citizen knows that these people get first priority off the assembly line and so, when a new line of fur hats comes out, the big shots identify themselves simply by wearing them.

In *For the Good of the Party*, Solzhenitsyn, who is one of the world's great journalists among his other talents, said in a wonderful piece of reportorial imagery, "Everyone knew the new arrivals were K.G.B. because they all wore pale-green fedoras."

If a consignment of fur hats arrives at GUM (State Department Store) or TsUM (Central Department Store), queues will immediately form half a mile long. To be more precise, three lines: one to select the hat for size; one forming at the cash desk to pay the bill; the third returning to the counter to present the receipt and take the hat.

This does not apply only to fur hats, of course. It applies to everything. One sometimes wonders dizzily when Muscovites find time to go to work at all.

Even so, keeping warm in the winter is less of a problem than one might expect, especially for a tourist. The head is the most important area to protect—I am convinced the cold can penetrate the skull and freeze the brain cells, and the result of that can be madness. Yet at two degrees above zero Fahrenheit I have found myself comfortable in Moscow in a light overcoat, fur hat, cashmere scarf and light Italian loafers, without recourse to any special underwear or even gloves. In fact, that was the temperature, and that is what I was wearing in Red Square, in the photo on the jacket of this book. And this in a cold that has to be experienced to be believed. Even Minneapolis and

Montreal are not so cold, and I have experienced winters in all three.

In Moscow it is so cold that the expression freezes on one's face. If you go out looking blah, you return looking blah. Try to smile in the middle of a city block, and your face cracks like glass. The tears that flow from the eyes freeze to the lashes, so that upper lash and lower lash are connected by icicles. The nose runs constantly. Charles IX of Sweden and the Emperor Napoleon both made the mistake of invading Russia in the summer. Had they had any experience of the country in winter they would not have tried in the first place.

It so happened I was doing business a while ago with Novosti, the *soi-distant* news agency, and so had pleasant social intercourse with Russians which under other circumstances would be impossible. I suggested with insufferable arrogance that the Russians had been figuring out their weather wrongly for the past thousand years. Walking briskly in light clothes is healthier than laboring slowly under the burden of kilos and kilos of fur, leather and wool.

My friends were too polite to tell me what they really thought of such fatuous inanity. They were even kind enough to say that I was not necessarily wrong. Merely irrelevant. The fact is that cold is cumulative. It can stimulate and animate for a week, or two weeks, or even three weeks. One feels as light as air and wants to run. But little by little the psychological and physical resistance weakens, and after eight months the Russians, purple-cheeked, gasping, blowing noses, weighed down with clothes, are exhausted and in no mood for stupid remarks like mine.

Learning to smatter in Russian is more important than learning to smatter in other languages. The Cyrillic alphabet is the easiest aspect of the problem—a paper tiger. It can be learned in half an hour. It is called Cyrillic after a tsar called Cyril who developed hiccups, and out came the Russian alphabet. It tends to be a problem in reverse; one starts thinking in Cyrillic. I landed once in Paris from Moscow thoroughly Cyrillicized, saw the sign *Homeopathie* over a pharmacy, and read it as *Nome-oratnniye*.

If one gets lost in the cold without means of communication, one is in the kind of mess that can lead to panic. There may be no shops in which to get warm. In Moscow, as elsewhere, the taxi is a slowly dying species, especially when most urgently needed. Thus necessity can make one quickly learn the basic words: yes, no, please, where, left, right, how much, how far. I once gave a bell-bottomed hick from Hickograd fluent directions to the Ploshchad Mayakovskovo (Mayakovsky Square). But Moscow is a complicated city, and I dispatched him in quite the wrong direction.

Moscow, as a city, is very similar to Washington, and it is easy to get lost in both. Each specializes in huge government administration buildings and heroic statues of struggling laborers. Both possess avenues so vast as to be almost trackless wastes. And I have a personal theory that both cities turn very slowly on a central axis, so that when one returns six months later, every street sign points in a slightly different direction, flummoxing the unwary traveler.

One of the secrets of Moscow, and one which must have contributed to the genius of Russian literature, is its conquest of time. No matter how busy one keeps oneself, there is always lots and lots of time left. One cannot go window shopping because all the windows are deep in cobwebs of frost. Despite the abundance of bookstores, there are none to browse in in the Western sense. They are drab shops packed to the doors with earnest Muscovites who know just what textbooks they want. Any book of general interest, including Dostoyevsky, is always sold out. Any new book by a popular author, hot, as the saying goes, off the presses, starts the inevitable queue of would-be readers.

One can buy the works of Marx and Lenin in dozens of different editions, from paperback to gold-leafed triple morocco, but nobody ever seems to, because they cram the shelves. I have never seen a set in any private Moscow home. Some works are unavailable period. They include the writings of Joseph Stalin and the thoughts of Mao Tse-tung.

Almost no course of action exists in Moscow that can be decided on a whim, not even "Let's go to the movies." Everything has to be planned well in advance. It sounds grim and daunting. In fact it is stimulating, and it is wonderfully clearing to the mind. It leaves one with time to solve one's own problems.

Theoretically it is possible to date an Intourist girl. The authorities actually take the possibility so seriously that they have published a heavy book for Intourist girls to study, and I saw a copy on my most recent visit. It is called *Handbook of Foreign Tourism in the U.S.S.R.* It has nearly eight hundred pages. Only two thousand copies were published, and each copy has a number and has to be signed out and returned.

The girl is informed that she must not under any circumstances "enter into any personal relationships with foreign tourists." She is permitted to give him her address if he wants to engage in correspondence later. The address is 16 Marx Prospect—headquarters of Intourist.

She is allowed to talk politics, providing she does not veer in the slightest from the party line. "The basic task [of the Intourist girl] is to give the foreign tourist a correct idea of the achievements of the Soviet people in the construction of a Communist society and of the peace-loving policy of the Soviet state."

An Intourist guide must be "unlimitedly devoted to our Fatherland."

She is allowed to smile—though she rarely does—but strictly not allowed to be flirtatious.

I have seen Americans try to be cheerful and informal with Intourist—a hopeless pursuit. If these words help future American tourists to desist from wasting their time, this book has not been wholly in vain.

Most people in Moscow, behind their façade of rudeness, are rather delightful and a little bit mad. From my eighth-floor hotel room at the National I watched, every day, a young secretary in an office across the way. She was pretty, wore a white babushka scarf around her head and, like all Russians, she possessed a passion for plants and flowers. She paid far more care to her inside garden of greenery than to her battered typewriter. She typed diligently while the boss was there. The moment he left the room, the girl quit the typewriter, the watering can came out, and all work was forgotten.

I could see her talking to the plants, smiling at them and sometimes even kissing them. She seemed to know the boss's comings and goings to a dot, or perhaps she heard the elevator reach the floor, because she darted back to her work seconds before he returned. He looked like a sour man, and I detected no rapport between them.

My butterfingered chambermaid came to me, sobbing. "Gospodin! Gospodin! I have broken something! Can you find it in your heart to forgive me?" She had dropped the aspirin bottle. I found it in my heart to forgive her and gave her an Estée Lauder lipstick. Next day she came back sobbing even harder. This time it was my Habit Rouge aftershave lotion from Guerlain in the Champs Elysées. We cried together this time, on each other's shoulders.

I went with a Russian friend, a language professor, and his twenty-year-old daughter to see *Snow Maiden* at the Stanislavsky Theater. It was bad. I was fascinated, because I never realized that Russian professionals can actually dance badly. At the two intermissions the three of us tore the performance to shreds, just as one would do on Broadway or in London's West End. At the end of the ballet the Snow Maiden marries her hero, and the sun comes out and melts her. As the curtain fell, I rose to beat the rush to the cloakroom, and then stopped. Huge tears rolled down the cheeks of my friend's daughter. My friend was blowing his nose loudly into his handkerchief. From all around me I heard muffled moos of grief. I felt that I had missed something, or else I was a soulless rotter.

The same Russian friend was bothered by the invasion of Americanisms into the Russian language. This is something comparatively new in the Soviet Union, although France has been unsuccessfully fighting *franglais* for years (remember *les buildings de grand standing*?). He told me with horror that Russian businessmen are now in the *import-eksport biznes*, and have to keep a good *balans* to avoid a financial *krizis*. The younger kids attend *djam sessions*, wearing *kovboiskie* shirts and *dzhinsy*. They *tvist* and *sheik*. My friend was upset about *populizm*, *nonkonformizm*, *détant*, *mass mediya* and *kheppening*. He said that, in his opinion, pro-Western snobbishness among Russian intellectuals puts Russia at a disadvantage in cultural competition with other nations.

In fact, the Russian language has always imported western terms: German and Dutch under Peter the Great, and French in the eighteenth and nineteenth centuries. A Russian salesgirl, berated and yelled at by her customers, will mop her brow, and say "*Kashmar*." The French word for "nightmare" is *cauchemar*. "Sidewalk" in Russian is *tratwar (trottoir)*, and a cloakroom is a *garderob*. Russians eat a snack which they call *butterbrod*. To acquire the steel teeth so many of them wear, they visit the *dantist*.

There are no usherettes in Moscow theaters, only old ladies in babushkas at the entrances who tear a little strip off your ticket. As usual, I had bought several tickets in advance and decided to see the Moiseyev company for a second time. I took the Metro to Mayakovsky Square—the Moscow subway is eight cents for any distance—and into the Tchaikovsky Theater, where the old babushka told me I should have gone to the Stanislavsky Theater.

I blasphemed and ran to the Stanislavsky, arriving just as the lights were going down. I could see only one empty seat, not quite my number but near enough, and sat down beside a pretty girl who regarded my presence with horror.

An American girl would have said, "Excuse me, but I think you're in the wrong seat." An English girl would have blasted you with a devastating "Do you *mind!*" (occasionally varied to "*Do* you mind!"). But Russians are too shy for that sort of thing. The lights went out. The orchestra started up on the overture to *Swan Lake.* I was in the wrong theater on the wrong night for the wrong show, with the wrong ticket. I don't know who squirmed harder through the first act, me or my accidental companion. I fled at intermission, and from a distance saw her bombard a wilting boy friend as though it were all *his* fault. I watched the rest of the performance standing.

In the foyer of the Bolshoi I encountered the great dancer Serge Lifar. Monsieur Lifar happens to be a neighbor of mine on the French Riviera. We chatted for a minute or so, and then he drifted on with friends. I plucked at the sleeve of an intelligent-looking young Russian and said, "That's Serge Lifar." He looked at me, uncomprehending. I pursued it. "Star of the Diaghilev Ballet." There was still no reaction. Nobody stared at Lifar, who certainly has one of the most unforgettable faces in all ballet history. I tried it on a couple of others. None seemed ever to have heard of Serge Lifar or, for that matter, of Serge Diaghilev.

Moscow can tear its landmarks to bits with just as much orgiastic relish as New York or Paris. Manhattan can gulp 277 Park Avenue and wash it down with Penn Station, but Moscow polishes off whole districts. The old aristocratic Arbat section has been ripped apart for a six-lane highway connecting the Kremlin to the Foreign Ministry. This is where Pushkin lived, where characters from Anton Chekhov, Tolstoy and *Dr. Zhivago* used to stroll in the summer evenings. Hundreds of stately homes of the Russian nobility have been razed. The beautiful Sobachya Ploshchkadka (Dog Place) where seventeenth-century tsars kenneled their hunting dogs, and ladies walked their house pets, Turgenyev-manner, has gone completely. They did move number 12 Composer Street to another site, however. Lenin lived there for four days in 1897.

In their place, to serve the vast avenue, has been built the "new Arbat," with a bank of high-rise apartment buildings, the lower floors devoted to restaurants, cafés, department stores "in the latest international style."

The official Intourist booklet promises even more. " 'Old Moscow' is only a drop in the sea of buildings that have been put up by Soviet architects. A new Moscow is being built—of broad avenues and spacious squares. . . ." In other words, you have been warned. If you want to go to Moscow, go there fast, or it won't be there anymore.

Moscow induces a certain hilarity in its foreigners. Rita Grosvenor, wife of a *Daily Express* correspondent, tells of some British electronics engineers who decided, after a bibulous night, to find the bugging equipment in their hotel rooms. They pulled up the carpet of one room, and there it was, a treacherous metal cap screwed to the floor. They applied a screwdriver. It came apart. They heard a muffled crash as the chandelier on the floor below fell, and gave up their search.

It is not *quite* true that *Pravda* and *Izvestiya* are unreadable. They do tend toward statistics and publishing speeches verbatim, which can often fill a whole page of a four-page paper. The photographers and picture editors of both publications should be fired. But in fact both papers give marvelous human insights into everyday life, items which the foreigner never expects, simply because the Russians are without so much that the Westerner takes for granted.

Not long ago *Pravda* reported that the Soviet Union, with its 250,000,000 people and an economic potential second only to that of the United States of America, has all of seven secretarial colleges.

Outside the go-go Novosti News Agency—of which much more later—the secretary as we know her scarcely exists. Nor does the receptionist. According to *Pravda*, even a senior executive or engineer has to spend up to 40 percent of his time doing simple and even menial office chores. He has to type his own letters, lick the stamps, and reach for the paste jar to seal his envelopes (Soviet envelopes do not include gum). If he has a business luncheon—and Russians do have business luncheons—he has to telephone the restaurant himself to reserve a table, confirm it with a note to the maître d'hôtel and find an office chauffeur to take the note to the restaurant.

The Soviet Union has always glorified heavy industry at the expense of everything else. Service jobs were despised and, being despised, attracted only people who were no good for anything else.

Pravda confirmed all this. It wrote, "Let us just start by seeing who would want to become a secretary in the first place. Such jobs as a rule are held by people without any special training or skills. If you ask them to be frank, many will admit that they view their job as a strictly temporary one, and they do not take it seriously."

One of the statistics the Russians like to trot out is that the Soviet Union turns out 2,650,000 graduate engineers a year, ten times more than the United States. But, *Pravda* admits forlornly, these same engineers spend nearly half their time doing work that could more conveniently be done by secretaries. *Pravda* mentioned one Ukrainian factory, the Heavy Machinery Plant in the city of Zhdanov, which had five thousand engineers and exactly 120 secretaries.

While I was last in Moscow *Pravda* declared Moscow restaurants to be "awful." "Even when skillful designers attempt to improve the dingy white-tile interiors of most Soviet cafés, surly waiters"—of which, again, much more later—"and menus, which don't carry any of the dishes they list, make eating out an ordeal, rather than the pleasure it ought to be in a city like Moscow."

The newspaper named specifically two cafés, the Musa and the Sadko, both of which had been redecorated in dramatic and tasteful decor, with wood-paneled walls, and color television. But at the Musa the service was slow, the food "awful" and the coffee undrinkable. Finally—I love this bit—the waiter told *Pravda*'s investigating reporter to finish quickly because he had not ordered enough to make service worthwhile.

At the Sadko everything on the menu was off, and only two items were available at the height of the luncheon period. One can safely hazard a guess that those two items were left only because nobody wanted them!

Curious, I tried the Musa, which, as *Pravda* said, was a very pleasant and airy place. After an hour's wait and a complete failure on my part to interest a waiter, I left. I decided to give the Sadko a miss.

Pepsi-Cola, the first American consumer product to go into mass production in the Soviet Union, has been a sellout, even at more than fifty cents a bottle. *Pravda* called it "a cooling beverage." However, it posed a problem. Pepsi-Cola has snob appeal. Buyers were not returning the bottles but keeping them as souvenirs, or to display rather ostentatiously on their sideboards, the way, in the West, we like to prove we have had Dom Perignon. This apparently is further aggravating the bottle shortage in the Soviet Union.

And for those who enjoy the triumph of good over bad, I have a pleasing morality tale to tell. The West has been recurringly horrified at the reports of political dissidents being sent to lunatic asylums by Soviet psychiatrists. Three names crop up again and again as the "baddies" in the picture, the psychiatrists who approve the sentencing. They are Daniel Lunts, Andrey Snezhnevsky and Georgy Morozov, and they seem to be the hatchet men for whatever line is laid down by their party masters.

I am callously delighted to report—on the authority of several

Moscow foreign correspondents—that they are now hoist by their own petard. As senior members of the Serbsky Institute of Psychiatry they are regularly and routinely invited to international psychiatry conventions. One can imagine how much they would love to go, and they would have no trouble getting official permission to leave the Soviet Union to attend, but they always decline.

They are sure that if they ever leave the safe stockade of their country they would never return alive. They are certain that they would be assassinated by the Jewish Defense League, and they probably would be, a possibility which leaves me—Christian though I like to consider myself—strangely unmoved.

I have suggested in this pastiche that people-watching in Moscow is completely different from people-watching in other parts of the world. It is not like people-watching in Paris, where one sits at a sidewalk café observing the passing drama of the human race. It is not like people-watching in Madrid, where one waits for friends to pass and hails them with a piercing "Psst!" (It has always been an inexplicable marvel of the Madrileño personality that *only* the person to whom the *"Psst!"* is directed turns and exclaims, "Hey! Pepe!" while all the other passersby keep going as if they have heard nothing.)

It is not like people-watching on the Via Veneto, where one seeks to spot aspiring starlets, or which new broad Sammy Davis, Jr., has on his arm. Veterans of the Via Veneto hold that girls always walk *down* the steep hill and never up it, thus providing more bounce to the ounce for any movie producer who may be outside sipping his Negroni. Nor is it like people-watching in Lisbon, where one tries to spot which of the passersby are Communists and which are Fascists. People-watching in Moscow has a totally different texture and intensity, strictly Russian. In the next chapter I shall be more precise.

2

A Quiet Night at the Metropole

It takes only one hot dinner session in the restaurant of the Metropole Hotel on Marx Prospect to turn a raw tourist into a hardened professional observer of Moscow life and society. There is an old-fashioned raffishness about the Metropole that exists nowhere else in Moscow, or in the Soviet Union for that matter. In Europe's most puritanical city, it carries a palpable air of sin, whores, kept women and unmentioned vices, symbolized on the broad staircase halfway up to the mezzanine by a large bronze statue of two naked children kissing each other in a manner far in advance of their tender years.

Western tourists tend to prefer the huge Rossiya Hotel with its neo-Hilton atmosphere, or the glass-box Intourist Hotel, with their modern innovations like giving the houseguest his key at the desk in the lobby, instead of having it handed over by the formidable lady sitting outside the elevator on each floor. Traditionalists prefer the cozy National, with its motherly waitresses and gilded ceilings (they were being regilded when I was last in Moscow, and the gilders were all old women). The Japanese tend to throng at the wedding-cake Stalinist Ukraina on Kutuzovsky Prospect. Because the Ukraina abuts one of the foreign compounds of Moscow, the lobby often resembles the bar at the United Nations.

The Metropole is not like any of these. It is somehow more

Russian, much more Moscowish. In the other hotels one feels like what one is: a foreign tourist among other tourists. At the Metropole one feels, in a masochistic kind of way, that one belongs. The Metropole is tatty and always smells of dust. Whether it is new dust or the same old dust I cannot tell, but after nearly a quarter of a century of visiting there is always that familiar smell of Metropole dust to make one feel one is home again.

The food in the Metropole restaurant is rotten, and it is amply matched by the service. The orchestra is atrocious. Why, then, do I keep returning to the good old Metropole, heart always beating in anticipation of unexpected excitement? And why do I almost never experience a letdown? The answer is that under the vast Victorian stained-glass dome one is likely to see more of Moscow high life and more of Moscow low life than in any other assembly place in the city. It is not easy to explain, but one can try.

The restaurant itself: In the center a marble fountain plays, and around the fountain couples dance. Behind the orchestra stage is a fine stained-glass window through which one can see, as in a Chinese shadow play, the old-fashioned hotel elevators rising and descending, and ghostly silhouettes going up and down stairs.

Determined on this particular evening to beat the posttheater rush from the Bolshoi across the road on Sverdlov Square, I arrived early. I actually found a table to myself, pushed back the dirty dishes left by the previous diners and sat down. The restaurant was as yet scarcely half full. The Metropole, however, is always ripe for the unexpected. I had scarcely sat down when a young blond thug in the black suit and clip-on bow tie of a maître d'hôtel swooped and handed me a greasy menu, the pages almost disintegrating from use. I knew the menu by heart. It has not been changed in a quarter of a century at least. What I had in mind to begin with was borscht. But the headwaiter, who was pushing caviar tonight, took the menu out of my hands and turned to the caviar page.

"Caviar, red or black?" he said, pointing.

"Borscht, please."

"Caviar."

"Borscht."

Flushed with rage, he summoned a colleague, and they both held the menu open at the caviar page.

"Caviar!"

"Borscht!"

"Caviar!"

"Borscht."

They conferred for a while about whether to serve me at all. Together they turned to the meat section, and two dirty forefingers impaled themselves on the fillet of beef. I said, "Chicken Kiev."

"Beef fillet."

"Chicken Kiev."

"Beef fillet."

"Chicken Kiev."

They conferred, looked at me, conferred again, and departed, snarling. The dirty dishes remained on the table. Relaxed, I settled down for a long wait. The waiters stood in clusters, chatting and smoking. They were young, and several had broken noses. They looked and behaved like graduates from reform school, and they were probably just that. In the rigidly stratified hierarchy of Soviet society it is almost impossible to sink lower, or earn less, than to wait on table.

Three tables away two immense peasants were exceedingly drunk on dark beer and vodka. One was astonishing, a veritable mountain of a man, with a disproportionately small head shaped like a carrot. He looked like the villain whom Popeye knocks out of sight after he has had his spinach. His double chin almost doubled the length of his face. He wore a brown suit with a tin badge in the lapel. He was probably no more than thirty.

At a table for two on my starboard bow a very pretty girl sat alone. She was eating a large order of smoked salmon which she fastidiously cut into dainty portions, and then ate American style, with the fork in the right hand. She looked very much like Jane Fonda. The blond thug of a maître d'hôtel stopped by several times to chat with her, ignoring incoming customers. He seemed to know her very well.

Then our young musicians in shirtsleeves mounted the music platform, making a lot of noise and smoking cigarettes. They chatted among themselves as though arguing over what to play and settled on "We All Live in a Yellow Submarine" at a beat which made one wonder, Who on earth hires these fellows? Presumably they must pass some sort of audition, so what kind of musical taste do the auditors possess?

The Popeye bruiser rose to his feet. And he rose. And he rose. It seemed he would never stop rising. He was at least six feet four inches, with a paunch to match, his tiny turnip of a head and balloon of a double chin emerging from a dirty open-necked shirt. Like a drunk trying to walk a straight line in a police station, he trod his way to Jane Fonda and, rolling his eyes invitingly, asked her to dance. Without even swallowing the smoked salmon in her mouth, she said something which I translated roughly as, "Get lost, buster." It took him a few seconds to assimilate the message. Then the penny dropped, he made a U-turn with some difficulty, and floundered back to his table. The chair almost came apart as he sat.

Jane Fonda was not to remain alone for long. A small, thin, swarthy man, with tango hips, Speedy Gonzalez sideburns and a tight suit, sat down opposite her. They lowered their heads and talked conspiratorially. His eyes flicked right and left as he talked, casing the customers, missing none. The eyes rested contemplatively and for quite a long time on the solitary me. I turned my head away, and he almost audibly snapped the shutter closed on me as a waste of his valuable time. From time to time they were joined by the maître d'hôtel, who stooped to join their conversation. They seemed to be asking him how was business, and I suspect they did not mean the hotel or restaurant business.

The room was filling up now. At the Metropole the more privileged diners sit at crescent-shaped leather banquettes surrounding the fountain and closest to the dancers. A party of three—a woman in her thirties and two men—was seated at one. She was slightly overweight but attractive, with a glorious complexion rare indeed in the harsh Russian climate. She looked like a young Barbara Stanwyck. One of the men, who seemed to be her husband, wore several badges of what seemed to me genuine distinction and importance. The other, younger but balding, had his back to me and seemed to occupy the traditional role of family friend. Barbara Stanwyck dabbed a brow which Victorian lady novelists might have described as alabaster. I saw that she had recently been crying. Her husband patted her hand on the table.

Next, the most handsome couple I have ever seen in Moscow sat at a table halfway between me and the bruiser and his friend (who was now asleep on the table). The couple would have turned heads on Fifth Avenue. The girl's chestnut hair was parted in the middle. She wore a neat print dress. Her handsome boy friend wore a gray chalk-striped suit and blue shirt. Only the plaid tie suggested that his access to fashion magazines was limited. He carried two windshield wipers—prestige symbols that indicated he owned a car. In Moscow car owners always remove their wipers; otherwise they would find them stolen when they returned to their car. The bruiser stared at the girl with glazed eyes, his eyebrows rising and falling like a monkey's. He hiccupped, with a hic that rattled the empty beer bottles stacked on his table.

My dirty dishes had not yet been removed. In the distant corner there was a brief flurry of violence as one of the waiters took a swing at another. He was quickly hustled, white-faced and angry, to the kitchen.

In the meantime Jane Fonda and Speedy Gonzalez had moved, for some reason, to a table in a far corner.

The beautiful couple had been efficiently presented with a

menu, and they ordered black caviar and Soviet champagne. They smiled fondly at each other. They liked each other a lot, and they were clearly not married. Contemplating the dirty dishes on my table, I wondered how long it would take for *them* to get their food.

Several of the diners were middle-aged or elderly Russians with young women. The women tended to be dumpy. They tended to yawn and look around them in an abstracted way, as though they could not wait for the night to end. One flaunted bright, lemon-yellow hair. On the floor the dancing was haphazard, following no discernible pattern. Although I am not one to talk, I noticed that not a single couple could be said to be dancing well.

At a table behind me three laughing North Koreans, all young, good-looking and well dressed, were eating chicken with their fingers. Suddenly they stopped laughing and seemed to freeze in their chairs. Two other Koreans had entered the restaurant, one probably in his forties, the other about fifteen, obviously father and son. The man possessed the most terrifying face I have ever seen in my life. It was a mask, like something out of an ancient Japanese print, with cropped, jet-black hair and a deep widow's peak. The eyebrows were clipped and pointed, like Mephistopheles, the eyes utterly without expression. He was Ian Fleming's Oddjob. He gave the impression that he spoke just seven words of English—"Ve haff vays of making you talk."

But even that was not the most frightening aspect of what I was witnessing. The son looked exactly like his father in miniature: the same widow's peak, pointed eyebrows, empty, lethal eyes. Both wore identical chocolate-brown suits and brown ties.

And they seemed to scare the three young Koreans as much as they scared me.

On the dance floor the couples increased and became more animated. The Muscovites are the easiest-going ballroom dancers in the world. The music means nothing. Waltz, quickstep, foxtrot—the Russians, if one will forgive the awful pun, take it in their stride. Bottom caroms off fat bottom; toe treads on instep. And some don't dance at all. They simply stand, clasped, moving their bottoms minimally. One young couple, he in an apple-green suit, apple-green shirt and dark-blue tie, she in a dark-green dress and green satin shoes, bowed deeply and formally from the waist before and after each dance. Several other couples danced gopaks. Others twisted. The orchestra played "I Did It My Way," which seemed to me to be singularly appropriate.

I suggested to a passing, sweating waiter that he might remove the dirty dishes, but he hurried past me on more urgent business, head averted. Barbara Stanwyck, between the two men, was in tears again. The husband looked tragically into space, his mouth twisting as he pulled on his black Russian cigarette. His medals gleamed under the chandeliers. The family friend looked down at the table, and then looked at the dancers without seeing them.

An elderly man, in sober Western dress, entered alone and looked around him in an abstracted manner. He spoke to the maître d'hôtel, who was all at once servile and rubbed his hands. The gentleman's lip movements and the good cut of his suit told me two things. He spoke Russian, but he wasn't Russian. He did not look like a Czech. I decided he was East German.

The huge bruiser was now swiveling around the ballroom, trying to find the toilet. I don't think I have ever seen such human mass, not even in a wrestling ring. He made the great Hackenschmidt seem svelte. He asked a waiter but apparently could not hear the answer because of the din of the orchestra, now playing "Cabaret." So the bruiser did a surprising thing. He lifted the waiter bodily and applied his ear to the hapless fellow's mouth. He then dropped him to the ground and the waiter fled, with a ghastly, terrified smile on his face.

The beautiful couple were eating their caviar, and ordered steak to follow.

The three young North Koreans, agitated, had succeeded in

attracting their waiter to pay their bill. They did not wait for coffee. They left in a fluster for the exit, keeping their eyes in front of them. The eyes of Oddjob and Oddjob Junior followed them out, and then they simultaneously resumed putting fork to mouth.

Barbara Stanwyck's husband was also weeping by now, and so, I think, was the family friend, whose back was toward me. Barbara leaned backward against the leather banquette to allow the two weeping men to bend over the table and kiss each other, their hands on each other's shoulders.

Meanwhile, Jane Fonda had left Speedy Gonzalez in the corner and was standing over the distinguished East German gentleman. I saw her lips move, and the lip-reading was easy. She said, "Is this seat taken? The restaurant is rather full." The East German half rose politely, napkin in his left hand. *"Pozhalvista"* he said, and the girl sat down, smiling at him and thanking him.

The Oddjob *père et fils* were now joined by an unexpected companion, a fair-haired, good-looking youngish man in the uniform of a lieutenant commander of the Soviet Navy. (In the Soviet Union and other Communist countries—even sophisticated Poland—it is considered acceptable to wear uniforms in private and on social occasions.) The two elders spoke. The boy listened impassively, eating rhythmically. Waiters who approached them were waved away impatiently. They spoke carefully to each other, with long pauses between every statement, as though each were weighing his words.

The bruiser's drinking companion, still asleep on the table, was now regurgitating, gently and unconsciously. I was happy for the beautiful couple that they sat with their backs toward this unsavory sight. Two men in quick succession asked the beautiful girl to dance, and she shook her head politely. One of them was me. The regurgitating Russian gave a loud snore. The beautiful couple turned and saw the two grotesques for the first time. The bruiser caught the girl's eye and gave her a lickerish smile from the side of his mouth. His teeth were as distressing as the rest of him. The couple turned back hastily and returned to their steak, smiling nervously to each other. The handsome young man, I noticed for the first time, carried a handkerchief in the cuff of his shirt, a somewhat foppish habit I had not seen in a very long time.

Barbara Stanwyck had risen, tragically, like someone saying goodbye for the last time. But she then moved into the arms of her husband to dance. Her movements were heavy; she was not a good dancer. She smiled at her husband bravely, put her wet cheek against his, and then I saw something that surprised me. Over her husband's shoulder, she gave the family friend, alone at the table, a huge wink. She briefly removed her right hand from her husband's shoulder blades to give the V for victory sign. The friend—and I—got the message. The poor cuckolded sod of a husband had been fooled by feminine tears.

The bruiser had removed his jacket, which made him, if possible, even more unappetizing than before. He wore a cheap shirt, cheap even by such Russian standards as exist, too tight for him, straining at the buttons like a cartoon character in Smilin' Jack.

Barbara Stanwyck, I decided as I watched her meat being heaved around the dance floor, could lose ten pounds and then be really attractive.

The beautiful couple did not dance, which made me believe that they were ballet dancers—or at least that she was. Ballet dancers never dance in ballrooms.

Zigzagging to avoid cerebral U-boats, the bruiser lurched over to the beautiful couple. Fat lips slobbering, double chin wobbling from side to side, he asked the beautiful girl to dance. Again she shook her head, looking frightened (at me she had merely looked uninterested). The effect of leaning forward to make the request was too much for the great elephant. He kept going, a good three hundred pounds of blubber, bones, booze and bad breath, and he hit the Oriental-tiled floor with a thud that shook glasses all over the ballroom. The beautiful girl screamed. The beautiful young man took her hand.

A sniggering waiter, cigarette in mouth, finally brought me my dinner. He pushed the dirty dishes to the other end of the table to make room for my caviar and fillet of beef, both of which I had refused to order, and both served at the same time. The caviar was opaque, without sheen, and looked as if it had been waiting for a customer for some time—I would judge about three days. The fillet of beef was cooked black and was cold. He also brought the little macédoine of peas and carrots in a basket of pastry which Intourist hotels seem to supply with every meal. They look great and taste strongly of the can they came in.

He offered a bottle of red wine (I had ordered white for my chicken Kiev). He also presented the bill at the same time. It was for four people and amounted to seventy-five dollars. He wished me *bon appetit* in Russian.

I hardly heard him. I was watching a good half dozen waiters trying to get the bruiser to his feet, but it was clear that they would have to send for the fire brigade or a forklift. The beautiful couple were laughing hysterically. The waiter drummed his fingertips on my table to attract my attention. He said, "Would you settle the bill now? And don't forget the tip."

3

Bottoms up in Moscow

It is Russia's joy to drink. We cannot do without it.

—St. Vladimir, 965–1015

The enemy of our life is alcoholism.

—*Sovietskaya Kultura*, September 24, 1974

It is an article of my faith that one can always get a drink anywhere in the world if one needs it badly enough, and one is prepared to work at it—in Toronto on a Sunday, in Jerusalem on a Saturday, in New York on election days, in Saudi Arabia during Ramadan, and in St. Peter's Cathedral if you ask any passing priest or Swiss Guard the way to the bar that is located there. My friend Brian Stratton, who has published his prison reminiscences, assures me that there is nothing easier than getting booze in the nick.

Bucking prohibition is easy, honorable, intellectually stimulating and part of the education fathers should be required to pass on to their sons. But to make drinking difficult in a city where alcohol is available everywhere in all sorts of succulent forms requires diabolical cunning. This Moscow has done, and does. In a country which distills the most aristocratic vodka on earth, the ordinary citizen has to go through every kind of stratagem to get it at all. Nothing I have come across in my travels around the world separates the men from the boys like the Moscow drinking test.

To begin with, there is the question of mixtures ("mix" as in "mixed drinks"). In a community like that of the Soviet Union, which produces everything alcoholic it wants and imports neither scotch, rye, bourbon, rum, gin, wine nor vermouth, the American drinker and the British Commonwealth drinker is faced with an important problem from the first moment he arrives.

Vodka he can get at once, from the Beryoska stores with his hard currency, but that is not the way the average Anglo-Saxon likes to drink. He does not simply drink alcohol for alcohol's sake. When presented with vodka, or indeed with alcohol in almost any form, he has a decision to make. He must arrive at his own separate solution of taste and pleasure. Study any American in any cocktail bar. He never grabs the glass the moment the bartender sets it before him. He studies it, circles it, weighs all the subtle permutations of blend, percentage and degree. He is a perfectionist who knows what he wants.

Given gin, he adds vermouth, or lime, or tonic or just a dash of angostura bitters to give it the delicacy of the drink known as pink gin. Into scotch whisky he puts soda or water, deciding— depending on whether he is American or British—whether to have it flow over ice cubes or directly into the glass. Given bourbon, he applies the purest of branch water; into vodka he pours the juice of orange. Or grapefruit to make a screwdriver. Or tomato to make a Bloody Mary. Or, before noon, cold bouillon to make a bullshot. He even spikes drinks which do not, by the nature of things, call for mixing at all: he laces champagne with brandy and bitters to make a French 75.

The British mix their beers in all sorts of permutations of taste and color. English soccer players have a taste for lager and lime—to an extent that frequently gets their names into the newspapers. The Irish add heavy cream and black coffee to their native whiskey, and I have just heard of a new New York concoction called B & B & T, which is brandy and Benedictine in thick cream added to tea.

The Russians would abhor such deviations. The Russians drink straight. This may seem a small difference of tradition, but for a serious drinking man there is no such thing as a "small difference." Every difference is basic, and the difference in Russian and Western drinking habits is as basic as the differences between our respective ideologies.

About a decade ago, before the Russians introduced hard-currency cocktail bars into the Intourist hotels, there was only one operative bar in the city, to the best of my knowledge. (Although one correspondent claimed he happened on one on the eighth floor of the Moskva Hotel, of whose existence even the management was unaware.) The official bar was in the Sovietskaya on the Leningradsky Prospect. Whenever I visited it it was closed and curtained off, but at least it was there.

A young American foreign correspondent, new to the ways of Moscow as they were then practiced, went to the length of trying to make a friend of the bartender. This is never an easy thing to do. The average guy behind a Moscow bar is on about the same social level as a restaurant waiter. He does not mix or blend. He simply pours out beer and vodka.

But the correspondent considered it worth a try. He instructed the barman to put a measure of Stalichnaya vodka into a pitcher of ice cubes.

"Tut!" he said at the smallness of the measure. "Make it a double."

He then ordered a touch of vermouth to be added—one sixth of the measure of the vodka—and for the delicate mixture to be stirred, not shaken, and poured in a smooth stream (to avoid bruising) over a single green Soviet olive.

He sipped the most noble of all cocktails and pronounced it magnificent. "You have invented the Moscowni, comrade," he said with emotion. "Your name will live in history, and you will receive much honor from the American press corps in this city."

Next day he returned, smacking his lips and rubbing his hands in eager expectation. "Same as yesterday," he cried.

The barman poured him a glass of Soviet port wine. That was not the same as he had had yesterday, the correspondent cried. Was it not? the bartender replied, picking his teeth. Yes, he recalled some gentleman or other coming in yesterday. Yes, he remembered mixing something or other, but he could not remember what. He had merely done as he was told. He had more to do (he implied) than cosset the alcoholic fantasies of foreigners.

Choking back his tears, the correspondent surrendered: "Give me a vodka."

This is example enough to illustrate that drinking in the capital of the Soviet Union is a completely different art form from drinking in the west—as different as the Russian language is from the English language. It has to be learned; hence these notes, historical, philosophical and practical, designed for future visitors to the Soviet Union who do not give a fig for the tomb of Lenin, or the delights of the Pushkin Museum, or the new Khrushchev memorial sculpted by Ernst Neizvestny, but care very seriously about the question of drinking.

First of all, there is only a handful of bars in Moscow, all situated in the Intourist hotels and exclusively reserved for foreigners. The drinks are exorbitantly expensive: beer is a dollar. Well-dressed Muscovites can often be seen drinking there, but only if they are guests of Westerners or pay in real money, not Monopoly-money rubles. Such Russians as do look in are turned away, and this often leads to noisy scenes. The Muscovite is an independent and truculent fellow despite a thousand years of tyranny and the knout, and he does not like to be pushed around. But, protest as he will, he will be chested out by a sneering maître d'hôtel as smoothly as if he were on the threshold of the Plaza.

The best bar in Moscow is the cocktail bar of the Hotel Rossiya, which is run strictly along New York lines. But the most interesting is the bar of the Bolshoi Theater. It serves no vodka, but it is considered *kulturny*—one of the most important words in Soviet society—to drink a glass of Soviet champagne, eat a chocolate éclair and stare at Soviet movie stars between acts.

There is a beautiful bar, in the great Victorian tradition, at the Hotel Metropole, but it is going completely to waste. It adjoins the restaurant and has wonderful cut-glass mirrors, beautiful chandeliers and a highly convenient footrail. I ventured to put a toe into it once and was indignantly waved away by the waiters. They use it as a stopping-off place between the kitchen and the restaurant, to puff on a clandestine cigarette and talk about their problems in life while allowing the food to get properly congealed. If one wants a drink there, one has to have it in the restaurant itself, on an off-white cloth medallioned in circles from red-wine bottles. This is what I mean by the Russians making it unnecessarily difficult for one simply to get a drink. And it never improves, from year to year.

The only indigenous Moscow cocktail until quite recently— such things are subject to change without notice—was something called a *koktel*. Perhaps it was a speciality of the Moskva Hotel roof garden, because it is only there that I saw it. (Usually every Moscow hotel serves the same food and the same drinks and shares the same shortages. If one hotel is without beer, they are all without beer; if one sees the refrigerator door open and bury the bartender in cans of beer, one can be certain that other bartenders in other hotels are being simultaneously buried in cans of beer.)

The *koktel* was a long drink, purplish and prefabricated, with a sort of vermouth base, I think. It was poured from big flagons into highball glasses, chunks of ice were added, and trolleyloads were wheeled around the tables in the evening by large ladies in spit curls, Cupid's bows and satin evening gowns. I tried one. All I can say about it is that it cost $2.50.

But the disappointments are compensated by the pleasant surprises. There are little champagne bars in most of the department stores, like GUM in Red Square. If one is prepared to buffet through the crowds of shoppers who seem happy to queue all day for practically anything, one discovers these half-hidden bars where chubby, unfriendly girls in white smocks and pale-blue berets dispense champagne by the glass. There is no pub-style jollity about the drinking: everyone drinks alone. Some customers sip their champagne, others down it bottoms up, bubbles and all. The latter tend to ask for refills. A medium-sized glass costs thirty-five kopeks, or about forty-five cents, and a good tumblerful costs double that. Soviet champagne is factory-manufactured, but that does not make it necessarily bad. No one would seek to make comparisons with the French or German product, but it is as good as any Italian spumante I know, as good as California champagne, and far, far better than anything made in the state of New York.

Yet drinking in Moscow, I am told by experts, is not what it used to be. Today we are conditioned to think that life in Moscow under Stalin was unmitigated hell and terror. I was surprised to find old Moscow hands talking nostalgically of the good old days of Stalin's tyranny, when everybody was drunk and happy from morning to night. For information on that golden era, I asked an Australian diplomat on his third tour of duty in Moscow.

Of Australians as diplomats I am not competent to speak, but as authorities on boozing they must at all times be listened to with the greatest of respect. He told me, "In the old days—now, alas, gone forever—we had the Koktel Hall on Gorky Street. It was run by the Moscow Vodka Trust, and the bartenders there were artists in the purest sense of the word. All cocktails had a base of either brandy or vodka, and the bartenders would lovingly fold in cream, or the whites of eggs, or both for that matter.

"They had a cocktail of their own invention called a *mayak*, perhaps the only non-American indigenous cocktail. *Mayak* means lighthouse, and it was well named. After even one of them your eyes flashed on and off in the dark and guided you home at night. Your head revolved in 360-degree circles, like that foul-mouthed little kid in *The Exorcist*. The *mayak* consisted of port, vodka, and cherry liqueur, or rather what the French call *cerises à l'eau de vie*, which is not quite the same thing, but better. Two blew your head right off. I am not exaggerating on this last point. I myself, with my own eyes, have seen at least five people leave Koktel Hall headless, great clouds of steam coming from where their neck used to be.

"When Stalin died the first thing the authorities did was to turn Koktel Hall into an ice-cream parlor. There was no announcement. The regulars went there one day as usual and found out that Koktel Hall was no more. The building still stands, and I often go there to look at it, just for old times' sake. It sometimes seems to me that the ghosts of drunks still stagger out at closing time."

"What about the open-air vodka carts which apparently have disappeared from the streets?" I asked.

He replied, "Don't stop me now, while I am going at full blast. There were beer halls all over the city. You bought a ticket from a lady in a black dress, took a large glass like an English pub's pint glass, stood in line and when your turn came they squirted it at you through a tube. You stepped over the drunks to find a table and drank your beer with black bread and salami. The beer wasn't so hot, but the ambience was terrific, watching the university students making a rush for the toilet before they threw up. Today there is a beer hall in the Hotel Ukrainskaya, and a few others around the place, and that seems to be the lot. It's very sad when you think about it."

"What about the open-air vodka carts which used to roam the streets?"

Barely controlling his emotion, my Australian informant went on, "In those days drunks staggered all over the streets of Moscow, magnificent specimens of alcoholism every one. Those who passed out in the Metros—the Metros were warm, you see— were picked up and trucked to a sobering-up station, which at peak hours resembled an advance medical station in the Battle of the Somme. They were sprayed with hot and cold water hoses, forced to touch their toes, then pummeled, given purgatives and hot and cold showers. Afterward they were shown the bill, which was as stiff as the roustabouts had been earlier. They were not asked to pay, however, because it was presumed they had drunk up their last kopek. It was taken automatically out of their pay envelopes at the end of the week."

So much for the golden days. The change began when Khrushchev visited Belgrade in 1955, got smashed at a public banquet and made a lunge for Madame Tito's bosom. Next morning he woke up groaning, decided that the Russians drank too much and that it had to stop. He raised the price of vodka and launched a nationwide campaign against alcoholism. The Russians responded valiantly to the campaign—they ate less bread in order to pay for their vodka.

But that was more than twenty years ago. Today vodka as well as brandy, the other staple Russian anesthetic, are almost priced out of the market. In a tour of the major gastronoms along Gorky Street and the Arbat I saw no vodka at all. Brandy cost a whopping ten dollars for a bottle somewhat smaller than an American fifth. Some time ago *Izvestia*, the government newspaper, accused Nedelya, the state liquor monopoly, of catering to the people's lowest drinking tastes. The paper alleged that the monopoly had shifted manufacture from high-quality table wines to fortified wines like port and Madeira. Failing vodka or brandy, these are what Muscovites buy in order to get drunk more quickly. The wines are measured in percentages, or degrees, of alcohol. At Russian Wines, the Gorky Street liquor store, customers simply asked, "Give me something at nineteen degrees," according to *Izvestia*. I bought a bottle of Soviet sherry there for $4.50. It wasn't bad. It wasn't good either.

The restrictions and shortages of liquor have encouraged all sorts of intriguing and highly imaginative forms of bootlegging. Any store which boosts its sales over a required norm receives a bonus from the state. An article in *Pravda* some time ago said candy stores, delicatessens, and even dairies sell vodka by the glass in order to lure customers.

In a city—a shriekingly cold city—where it is all but impossible to duck into a bar for a glass of liquid warmth (and even if one can, one must go through the compulsory ritual of leaving hat, coat, gloves, briefcase in the cloakroom), it was a perfect excuse to take a drink and buy a bar of chocolate at the same time. *Pravda* estimated that the vodka represented about 25 percent of the sales in these shops. One would think that it would be the easiest thing to spot, and it is completely illegal. But who is going to give the game away? Certainly not the half-frozen fuzz on traffic duty.

All Russian beer is ghastly, and they brew a Russian porter which they call **портер**. This is the worst of all. But they occasionally import gorgeous Czech beer which, after Ballantine's India Pale Ale, is the finest beer on earth. There used to be an imitation Coca Cola called *siyani*, but even before the arrival of the genuine Pepsi I never found anyone who drank it. I am told on good authority that the Russians manufacture a whiskey called *visky*.

Some of the Russian wines are very good indeed. All the vodka, of course, is magnificent and very strong, and there are variations of it that are little known in the West. *Tminaya* vodka has a caraway flavor. There is a lemon vodka. Pepper vodka, which is flavored with pimientos, brought back curious memories of my youth on the Lower East Side of New York. I used to watch the Bowery drunks, under the shade of the el, add red pepper to their rotgut gin. It gave the drink more bite and made them drunk quicker. It was intriguing to discover this link between the lushes of Skid Row and the lushes of Gorky Street. The latter drink the real thing, the former improvise. It is as unexpected, say, as going into a village in darkest Transylvania and finding that the peasants add homemade vermouth to homemade whisky to make a passable dry Manhattan.

There is a marvelous vodka with the enchanting name of *zveroboy* (animal-killer, or St. John's Wart). There is also

Khotnichnaya (hunters) vodka. The Ukraine produces a caramel-colored vodka called *yubileynaya* (jubilee). This, I was told, is Brezhnev's favorite, which means I move in important company.

But now we return to my original theme of what to put in the vodka; the heck with when in Moscow do as the Muscovites do. I'm no damn Cossack, and I don't like my vodka straight. On my latest trip to Moscow there did not seem to be a can of grapefruit or orange juice in the city. There was mango juice, though. The Trade Ministry had bought enough of the guck from Hyderabad to keep another siege of Leningrad going on mango juice alone.

I bought a can as an experiment, because I am very fond of fresh mangoes, a taste acquired in my years in the Philippines, and anyway there was no alternative. The girl behind the cash desk looked up from her abacus, amazed, and bawled at the floorwalker something that sounded like, *"Guv, vigotr idavon tlast."* The floorwalker recoiled a pace and bawled back *"Zwonbaun evrim innit."* I translated this exchange as, "Guv, we got rid of one at last," and the reply, "There's one born every minute."

I took it home to the Hotel National, where to get a can opener from room service took no more than a day or two. Alone, the mango juice tasted vile. With vodka it tasted worse, so I poured it over the waterbug in my bathtub and watched the insect's death agonies. I flushed the creature away before it occurred to me that I might have offered it to one of the Japanese Mitsubishi salesmen on the third floor as a delicacy.

Then one day, through the frosted glass in the GUM windows, I distinctly saw piled cans of Greek orange juice. Thrilled, I flung into the shop and lined up to buy the sales chit which one takes to the sales counter. I did not have to wait for more than twenty minutes, and read *Humanité* as I edged along (the only consolation about being obliged to read Communist papers in Moscow is that they can't cheat on the sports results; they don't dare say that Metrevelli, the Russian tennis star, won when he didn't). The girl took my rubles and gave me my chit. I then waited for another twenty minutes, doing the *Humanité* crossword, for my turn to purchase. To the fat saleslady I said, *"Sok appelsin."* *Sok* is juice. *Appelsin*, in Russian, as in German, is orange.

"Only mango juice," the saleslady said.

Forlorn, I went away and stood in line for an hour or so to get my money back, and even read the *Humanité* editorial. So I laced my vodka with what the hotel administration called "breakfast fruit juice," a kind of liquid jam. Tourists can't be purists.

The hard-currency cocktail bars in the big hotels have made life much easier for the serious drinker, but I am endlessly intrigued by one of the many oddities of Moscow life. The two traditional hotels of Moscow are the National and the Metropole, followed by the Berlin (formerly the Savoy). Hotels like the Rossiya and Intourist I consider Johnnies-come-lately. The hotels come under the same central direction and have identical menus. One would think they would be at least roughly similar, like, say, Steak'n'Brews or Howard Johnsons. Not a bit of it.

I have already described the unique ambience of the Metropole Restaurant, completely different from the tearoom atmosphere of the National. The same difference applies to the two Intourist bars in the two hotels. The National is quiet, tastefully lit, rather dull, very expensive, full of Japanese businessmen talking business to Italian motor executives from Fiat-Zhiguli, or counting the rubles they have just made from selling their spare suits to young Russians in the street outside.

The bar of the Metropole is something else altogether. It is right out of the Reeperbahn of Hamburg. Pop music blasts the ear. The bartenders look like chuckers-out with long service in the Soviet Merchant Marine. Tattoos in Cyrillic adorn their hairy forearms. And in the shadows dubious-looking girls with bright-yellow hair talk in fractured German to tipsy Swedes. And some people go home saying that they found Moscow dull!

The problem with one's Moscow friends then is not what to drink, because they will drink anything alcoholic, but how to drink. This is a problem to consider seriously, because the traditional habit of bottoms-upping can be lethal. The Georgians, for example, have seven basic toasts, all of which have to be honored before they let their imagination take sway, as it were. And they can reach the stage where they are toasting your maternal grandfather's third cousin twice removed.

Furthermore, Georgian toast glasses are pointed at the base, so they have to be set on the table upside down. This ensures that no one is chickening out by merely sipping. All this makes Swedish drinking, with its rigid ritual of skoaling, a game for children. Western diplomats in Moscow are warned in advance to gobble hors d'oeuvre between toasts to sop up the fusel oil in their systems; otherwise they would never survive. It is instructive to notice that all diplomats back from the Soviet Union have, without exception, put on an average of ten to fifteen pounds, and have only the vaguest recollection of their tour of duty. It is a sobering thought.

Soviet officialdom does not like the nation's reputation for drunkenness. Whereas it usually prefers to hide from the public the unpleasanter sides of Soviet life, like crime and accidents, it is constantly tearing its hair about what a bunch of lushes the Russians are. About a year ago *Izvestia* quoted with approval a new textbook called *Cocktails, Punches, Wines and Other Beverages*, by an economist called Alexey Mituikov. *Izvestia* said primly that it was not merely a collection of recipes for mixed drinks "but a sort of textbook for good drinking manners, and containing much useful and practical advice. . . . For example, it points out that champagne should not be kept in a refrigerator, because it becomes less 'bubbly.' On the other hand, it should not be warm, because in that case it becomes too lively, and there is a danger that it will spurt out of the bottle and drench the guests. Exploding bottles and flying corks are not usually considered a mark of good breeding." Professor Mituikov adds, however, that "this rule might be ignored in a small family circle."

After some basic advice on which wine to serve with different dishes—"white with fish, red with meat," and so on—

the professor concludes with this advice: "Remember that you should eat first and then wash down what you have eaten with wine, not drink up all the wine first and gobble all the food afterward."

Sounds like a pretty good book. I looked for it in the bookshops, but could only find the works of Marx and Lenin.

I was dining one night at the Aragvy Restaurant with Sig Shore, the New York movie distributor, when we were interrupted by four quite elegant young Russians dining at the next table. One of them said, "Excuse me for hearing your conversation, gentlemen, but we have previously learned some bad news. Is it true that Stamp Kempton is dead?"

Shore said, "You mean Stan Kenton?"

"Yes. Stamp Kempton, the jazz player."

"No, he's not dead. Unless he has croaked since I have been in Moscow."

The Muscovite's face lit up. Excitedly he relayed the message. The four hugged each other in joy, shook Sig's hand, shook my hand and ordered vodka for all. "We had heard he was dead," the first young Muscovite said. "We are very happy the report was exaggerated. I can't remember where we got the report. It couldn't have been on the B.B.C."

Shyly he proffered another name, and it startled us both. "What do you think of Joe Morello?"

This was a game for specialists indeed! Shore, an expert, could scarcely believe that a Muscovite could be familiar with the drums of Joe Morello. Intrigued, Shore tossed into the conversation the name of someone I had never heard of, a West Coast trumpet player called Shorty Rogers.

"Shorty Rogers!" the four exclaimed as one, and the party was swinging.

A stream of names came out, Symphony Syd, Cannonball Adderley, Ray Brown—names known to the élite of the world of jazz. I was lost halfway through, but Sig Shore was not once able to catch the Russians out.

I don't know whether the end was anticlimactic, but I am

inclined to think not. The four Russians were musicians in the orchestra of the Bolshoi, who played *Swan Lake* and *Eugene Onegin* all evening and listened to jazz all night. Not until the Aragvy turned out its lights did we end the memorable conversation. We shook hands outside in the snow, and the Russians went off to listen to more jazz on their transistors and tape recorders.

It was one of the happiest of many happy chance encounters in Moscow, but the next morning I did not feel so euphoric. I staggered to Moscow Airport and took an Ilyushin to Budapest. The Russian sitting next to me passed me his bottle of vodka, which I declined with a shudder. Budapest is also a Communist city, but, unlike Moscow, one would scarcely notice. With the bright lights, the boutiques and well-coiffed women, it is more like Vienna or Munich. Behind the cocktail bar of the Hotel Royal were arrayed rows of bottles of Tanqueray gin, Pimms Number One Cup, famous scotches, Italian vermouth. By now my spirit had been broken by the rigors of drinking in Moscow. Timidly, almost humbly, I asked, "I don't suppose you know how to make a dry martini?"

The bartender regarded me with contempt and set up a martini as crisp as one could get in Mike Manuche's, New York— and New York, after all, is the dry martini capital of the globe, along with San Francisco. After two I learned his name was Denec. After three, that he was a soccer fan. Next day he erected a flask of martinis and we went to see MTK Budapest play Ferencvaros. I forget who won, but I wager all Lombard Street to a China orange that there were not many other people in the crowd of forty thousand drinking dry martinis.

It was fine, splendid, scrumptious—but something was wrong, and I was unable to define what. In Paris the bar of the Hotel Crillon held no pleasure for me, save for seeing old friends still sitting in places they occupied before I went to Moscow. I found London pubs a bore. Then one evening I was drinking in the bar of the Wig and Pen in the Strand with a fellow called Brittenden.

"Brittenden," I cried. "Let's drink to Evonne Goolagong!"

"Are you out of your lower-middle-class Anglo-wop mind?" Brittenden demanded, not without reason.

"Let's drink to the Common Market," I said sullenly.

"I think I want to throw up," said Brittenden.

"All right, let's drink to Joe Morello."

"Who's Joe Morello?"

"All right, let's drink to the Queen, God bless her."

"I did that last night."

At that moment I wished, as I wish very frequently, that I were back in Moscow.

4

A Picnic in the Country

Soviet and Canadian Jews scuffled with police yesterday at a picnic outside Moscow, when police tried to pull down a small Israeli flag. After some pushing and shoving the police withdrew, Jewish sources said.

—Associated Press, September 22, 1975

Muscovites have a passion for their countryside. Winter, fall or summer, an afternoon's escape from the capital gives them a real feeling of spiritual achievement. It is a three-season constitutional—in spring it is almost impossible. The melting snow turns the countryside into a sea of impenetrable mud. Villages become isolated for weeks, and the villagers are dependent on radio for what passes in the Soviet Union for news.

The countryside has none of the variety or lushness one finds throughout Western Europe and outside most American cities. Western observers are convinced that the architecture of Moscow has something to do with this primal urge to go out of the city. Moscow always liked vast buildings, but today's Moscow is Stalin's memorial. He widened already wide boulevards and created squares large enough to accommodate five football games at once. The statues became bigger than ever. As the world's number one dictator, he could do what he wanted, and like most dictators he did not give a damn about history. The tyrant always considers he *is* history.

To the north of the city he demolished the beautiful 1812 Arch of Triumph, as well as monasteries and churches, and covered the lot with tarmac. He invented ring roads before Robert Moses or the Greater London Council did. For a city almost without cars he built a sixteen-lane highway around the city, at one point only a mile and a half from the Kremlin. Not satisfied, he built another, half a mile closer and wide enough to serve as a landing strip. From the wedding-cake skyscrapers to the palatial subway, this city is Stalingrad. And the only answer for the denizens who live in it is . . . escape.

In the country, even among stubbly fields, stringy trees and monotonous views, they at least feel like human beings. So my first invitation to a Sunday picnic in the country was not one to be declined. Several of the resident American correspondents, with their wives, children and dogs, were all going in a convoy of cars to Abramtsevo. They were inviting a few visiting correspondents, and would I care to come along? Would I!

The party consisted of Peter and Palmyra Gall of McGraw-Hill in general, and *Business Week* in particular, in their Zhiguli Fiat (Russian-built, and for which they had high praise), Liz and John Shaw of *Time*, and Hedrick and Ann Smith of *The New York Times*. These and their half dozen children formed the hard core of the Moscow permanent residents on the picnic. The marginals consisted of myself, the chess correspondent of *The New York Times* (in Moscow to cover the playoff tournament between Victor Korchnoy and Anatoly Karpov for the world championship title then held by Bobby Fisher), and the ice-hockey correspondent of Time-Life (in Moscow for the world championship series being played between the national teams of Canada and the Soviet Union).

Abramtsevo, our destination, is a small village about fifty kilometers outside Moscow and ten kilometers before Zagorks. It was the center of important art movements in the eighteenth and nineteenth centuries. We drove out of the city by Mir (Peace) Prospect, past the awful, but impressively awful, Monument to Space Conquerors.

The traffic of private motor cars was surprisingly heavy. Peter Gall, fluent in Russian, unassumingly intellectual and, in common with most McGraw-Hill luminaries, profoundly bearded, told me that the automobile had become the government's almost desperate incentive to increased output. Productivity in the Soviet Union, he explained, was abysmal. Money buys nothing but junk. Clock-watching, featherbedding, time-wasting and coffee-breaking are practices more rigidly adhered to than even in England.

The commissars had hit on two rewards for good work: meat and motorcars. One of the reasons, Gall said, for the frantic grain-buying by the Soviet Union was to keep the beef herds well fed. Work of Stakhanovite proportions earned an automobile, and on this Sunday morning it seemed that all good workers were on their way to Abramtsevo.

After getting a car, of course, one must learn how to drive it, and these workers seem to be taking an unconscionable time about it. The swerving and tailgating were alarming. In December 1974, for the first time, *Pravda* released the casualty figures for Moscow traffic accidents. It reported that 574 persons were killed and 5914 were injured in 1973. The total population of Moscow is about 7 million.

Comparison was made with London: the British capital, with an only slightly larger population, reported 697 traffic fatalities and slightly fewer than 8000 injuries in the same year. But London had 2.3 million registered automobiles in that year while Moscow had a mere 160,000—all these are *Pravda* statistics. Furthermore, London has 8000 miles of roads, while Moscow has only 1800 miles. This is making a little go an awfully long way!

Again we quote *Pravda:* only one third of private drivers have received satisfactory driver training. Car owners are numbered at 2 million in a nation of 250 million—fewer than in London alone. There are almost no training schools, and Russians finding themselves with cars have to ask friendly truck drivers to teach them what those pedals on the floor are for.

As in the United States, most road accidents are attributed to drunken driving, excessive speed, poor highway design and unsafe cars, but according to Peter Gall, who drives his car everywhere in Moscow, there are significant differences. Street lighting in the city is hopelessly inadequate, as are traffic signals, so that driving by night is a dangerous game.

As we travelled, stopping every few minutes at level crossings for innumerable trains, the chess correspondent talked chess with Hedrick Smith, comparing the skills of Petrosian to those of Kavelek, and Smith kept up with him in impressive fashion (the chess correspondent had beaten Bobby Fischer). Even before we left the city limits little wooden tsarist cottages began to appear in endless lines on each side of the highway. They were almost identical in construction: the door on the side, and a little carved central loft window under the eaves. Some were gaily painted in pastel colors, others pathetically ill maintained, with broken windows and sagging gates. Each village, no matter how small, displayed its heroic statue of Lenin on a plinth where, presumably, Christ or the Virgin stood before the Revolution. Each had its onion-domed church, every one in beautiful condition, kept that way by elderly ladies standing on ladders doing the gold leafing. Most were open and operating.

We turned off the main Zagorsk highway, and by a succession of Sleepy Hollow valleys, ponds, streams, cows, goats, and extraordinarily well disciplined geese, we arrived at Abramtsevo. I had an immediate feeling of *déjà vu*, although I couldn't then define it. In the record-breaking October sunshine the little hamlet—it was almost too small to call a village—was crowded with visitors, mostly young and all Russian except us.

The adventures began as soon as we had spread the blanket and opened the picnic baskets. Our possessions included a football, a Frisbee, two soccer balls, a baseball bat, a kite, a baseball mitt and a terrier called Amy. The New York Times provided fried chicken and raw carrots. McGraw-Hill supplied sandwiches on whole-wheat bread, salami and chocolate cake.

Time provided piroshkis of two kinds: meat and cheese. There was wine, beer, vodka. I, the visitor from warmer climes, contributed a bottle of Pernod, which made John Shaw very emotional about the French Riviera.

But we were not relaxed. A little old man was hovering a few yards away. His expression was one of noticeable malevolence. He wore an overcoat and a battered hat, and he reminded me of a diminutive Bill Sykes from *Oliver Twist*. .

Smith, an extremely tall, handsome man, almost oozing scholarship said, "I sense trouble."

The old man, however, had turned to chase away a group of children amusing themselves by making a cave in a haystack. He then focused his attention on a young couple kissing on a mound of new-mown hay. They got up and left.

"Our turn next," said Shaw.

"Typical Soviet busybody," said Gall. "Loves to throw his weight around. The system encourages it."

"Look at his indirect, diagonal approach," said the chess correspondent. "It reminds me of the Nimzo-Indian Defense as played by Spassky."

We outsiders decided to leave it to Smith, Shaw and Gall, the Soviet professionals. I asked the chess correspondent, "Anything in the news?"

"No," he replied, his eyes, like mine, on the sinister old Russian. "Today's a rest day. Karpov and Korchnoy aren't playing."

"I mean general news. Has war been declared, or anything of that nature?"

"I wouldn't know. I only read chess."

We tried to ignore the old man. Shaw and I, the two Britons, gave somewhat creaky soccer lessons to the American boys. Amy, the terrier, chased a goat. The old man finally reached us and told us to blow. Smith, Shaw and Gall gathered and poured over him a formidable concentration of Western intellect in the Russian language. The old bully wilted, and his manner changed. He said—I translate freely—"It's not my fault, guv, it's the boss. A proper Tartar 'e is. Cor blimey, 'e'll give me the full Siberia bit if 'e sees you 'ere enjoying yourself like capitalists. It's more than my job's worth."

Intellect opened its mouth to devastate, when something strange happened. The bully, now so unctuous, had flung out his hands in appeal. All four fingers and the thumb of his left hand were missing. Thirty years earlier he was presumably a young man and a soldier in the war that killed 20 million Russians. Intellect stopped. Silently we packed our picnic, assembled the children, collected Amy, got the Frisbee out of a thicket and kicked the soccer balls a hundred yards away to another site beside a pond.

Like the others, I said nothing, but a thought as unworthy as I can imagine would not go out of my mind—one of the troubles about being a writer. Imagination takes over, and fantasies dominate logic. The little old man, bullying the children, chivvying the young lovers and then groveling before his superiors, had had part of his left hand blown off in the war. In the terror of war, a bullet through the left hand, or foot, is the traditional self-inflicted wound. It is distrusted by all commanders and can lead to court-martial and punishment unless it can be established as legitimate.

I put the thought out of my mind. The October sun glowed as it would in Vermont on foliage of classical rust and red, on cheekbones kissed with latter-day suntans. Jackets were shed. This little corner of the countryside has inspired more great literature than any other place on earth. Even the chess correspondent paused in the middle of defining the Catalàn Opening to admit that it was a lovely day. The Frisbee flew, and so did the kite.

By the pond an elderly gentleman wearing a beret stood at an easel, painting in oil. A middle-aged lady wearing the sort of felt hat favored by Middle European ladies took photographs of us. Peter Gall noticed that she wasted half a roll before she realized she had left the cap on the lens. We laughed. She photographed us laughing, and scowled. We were joined by Philip Shorr, Moscow correspondent of the B.B.C., with wife and child.

Despite the warmth, the young Russians around us were heavily dressed, in woolen hats and stockings. "Russians are set in their seasonal ways," said Peter Gall. "It is October. Ergo, it should be cold, and they react accordingly."

A young Russian said something to Shaw. "He wants to know where you got your jump suit," Shaw told me.

"Joel McKay, Pasadena, California."

The reply spread around the Russians, and they gave me the thumbs-up seal of approval.

Still the feeling of having been here before persisted, and I could not put my finger on it. About a hundred yards away a group of young Russians of both sexes were playing soccer, the girls in goal and taking the job with great seriousness.

The encyclopedic Hedrick Smith gave us a lecture on Russian art. Russian reverence for oil paints, he said, was a factor for the constriction of Soviet art, quite apart from censorship. Artists were reluctant to waste oils on an abstract. For this reason Russian artists who sought to experiment in their work chose the lithograph as their form. Critics and censors considered the lithograph beneath their dignity, not worth attacking.

"Would you say," the chess correspondent asked, "that the lithograph is to Russian art what the Benko Gambit is to chess?"

"An interesting analogy," Smith conceded politely, and the chess correspondent looked pleased.

Smith then led us on a tour of the little commune. It was designed as an art and literary colony in the 1870s by one Sava Mamontov, a retired railroad tycoon and patron of the arts. Little dachas were built, and a workshop. Turgenev worked there. Gogol read the first chapters of *Dead Souls* to his friends there. (I *do* dislike authors who read their works to friends, don't you?) Chaliapin sang. They built a tiny church based on the Novgorod twelfth-century churches—locked, although it was Sunday and the commune was animated with several hundred tourists.

In the main house there was an exhibition of sixty contemporary lithographs by a painter called Nikolayevitch Goryayev, who had evidently visited the United States. One of the lithographs was an uncompromising abstract that reminded the chess correspondent of the Dragon Sicilian attack.

Smith accosted one of the lady curators, and she reported that visitors had more than tripled in number over the past three years, nearly all Russian and mostly young, and that they were becoming increasingly interested in their national history. Then the feeling of seeing it all before clicked into place, even down to the little old man.

Doylestown, Pennsylvania! I had been given a parking ticket by a petty tyrant even as I was starting the engine of my car to drive away. I had been visiting the Mercer Museum in that prettiest of Pennsylvania towns. Henry Mercer, a rich archeologist, antiquarian and inventor, in more or less the same period as Sava Mamontov, manufactured ceramic tiles, just as some of the artists of Abramtsevo did. As an amateur architect, Mercer was something of an eccentric genius, and he pioneered in concrete construction. Three major monuments remain as a testament to his genius. One is the Mercer Museum in Doylestown, built in concrete in the style of a French chateau. It houses a magnificent collection of early Americana, wagons, coaches, fire engines, craftsmen's equipment. The visitors to the Mercer Museum, like the visitors to Abramtsevo, tend to be young, and they ask many questions. The second monument is his equally spectacular factory, built in the style of a Spanish monastery. Here, his skilled and cruelly underpaid workmen worked seven days a week. For himself he built his third monument, a fantastic private mansion, a few hundred yards away from the factory, in the middle of a cultivated park. It looks like a smaller

Neuschwanstein, and he called it Fonthill, presumably after Wyatt's folly in Kent, England.

Both Mamontov and Mercer were rich businessmen, both absorbed in the history of their respective countries, one creating his legacy just outside of Moscow, the other a similar distance from New York. What first struck me as soon as I arrived at Abramtsevo, and which I could not immediately define, was that the visitors there reminded me of the visitors to the Mercer creations: same age group, same sense of national pride and a kind of wonderment. Even the area of their interest was identical—their respective countries' historical tradition. There must be plenty of morals to draw from this intriguing parallel, but I can't think of a single one. It is simply there.

The point has been made, and the significance of the countryside for the Russians had become clearer to me. As countryside it is not up to much. But, as I have suggested elsewhere, everything about Moscow, whether tsarist, Stalinist or post-Stalinist, is designed to hammer into Muscovites the sense of their own insignificance. They need the countryside because of emotional forces that do not exist in the West. Denied the right to a soul in Moscow, they find it outside, every weekend.

5

Crime in the City

Sooner or later every traveler to Moscow, without exception, will be approached near his hotel or in Red Square by young men asking to buy clothes, change money or dispose of anything he does not need, from razor blades to Hush Puppies. As the reader will learn later, there is even a market for the birth-control pill. In appearance these young men are not the kind to give rugged free enterprise a good name. They are invariably seedy fellows with shifty eyes, like the ones who offer to sell you a watch on the stairs of the Forty-second Street subway station at Eighth Avenue. They have a not unnatural tendency to shiver as they stamp their beat looking out for foreigners and the police.

They are breaking all sorts of laws and so, technically, is the visitor who deals with them. Some of them, of course, are police plants. If the turns and quivers of Soviet foreign policy make it convenient for them to embarrass West Germany, the K.G.B. will instruct its seedy young men to concentrate on German tourists. And sometimes it becomes the turn of the British or the Americans.

But the record of organized crime in the Soviet Union is as staggering as anything in the United States, and, as in the United States, it has its roots in the economic system itself, thriving on the system's flaws.

The empire of Jan Rokotov came to an end as long ago as 1961, but the sociological significance of Rokotov remains as great as that of Al Capone. Five years earlier Khrushchev had denounced Stalin at the famous Twentieth Congress. It was the beginning of an era, still continuing, when blinkers began to fall from the eyes of the Russian people, showing them a world that many did not want to know existed.

Jan Rokotov called his huge gang the League of Lucky Gentlemen. He liked to be addressed by his henchmen as "King"—in English. While his fortunes prospered—and they prospered for an impressively long time—life was very good indeed: cars, pretty girls, parties which were lavish even by Russian standards, vacations on the Black Sea coast and the Crimea. Money poured in on him: rubles, dollars, marks, pounds.

From Moscow Ralph Parker, mentioned elsewhere, stated in the British *New Statesman* that Rokotov was a financial genius, nothing less. That genius is what makes him unique in the history of crime, as the Communists understand the word. Rokotov was an organizer of extraordinary ability and flair. He could handle people, knew when to delegate and how to make decisions. Had he grown up in Britain he might have acquired, in time, a genuine title, and been acclaimed in the business pages of the newspapers like Slater, Poulson and Kornfeld. In America he could have risen to the top of a multinational corporation. In a bad year he might have been elected Vice President.

Rokotov was only thirty-four years old when he was finally caught. Even then it was not by the wits of the police, but by betrayal by an Iago in his own court.

He was born in Moscow of working-class parents. By the time he left school he had amassed, through schoolboy trading, a ruble fortune amounting to more than a thousand dollars. As a reward for this capitalist initiative he was sent to prison on charges of "speculating," a foolish move on the part of the authorities because he came out of jail richer than when he went in. He discovered that many of his fellow prisoners were

Moslems, and considered the possibilities for a while. Then he worked out a little scheme to pay them for their pork rations and sell the meat, at a handsome profit, to the guards.

Rokotov's return to freedom—if the Soviet system can be called freedom—coincided with Nikita Khrushchev's declared policy of opening Russia up to Western countries as a tourist attraction, thereby garnering important foreign currency reserves.

To the Russians, deprived of even the simplest luxuries, famished not only for material goods but also for any kind of cultural contact, the arrival of the first travelers from the West must have seemed like a visitation from another world. As long as *everybody* wore shapeless jackets, bell-bottom trousers and self-service haircuts, nobody cared. But the sight of elegant foreigners in smart suits and dresses turned the mirror on themselves and made them feel ashamed. They began to pine to belong to this refined community.

But they were separated from the visitors by everything the Soviet state could devise. They were discouraged from fraternizing; indeed, they could be arrested for it. The newspaper campaigns against the horrors of life in the capitalist countries were intensified. And all the time a man's suit of reject quality by American standards cost $160 at GUM, and incredibly inferior shoes cost $40.

The Soviet system is inherently antimoney. It does not like or understand money. Factories produce, food is grown, men conquer space, supersonic airliners are designed—all without any real conception of profit, loss and budgeting costs as the West knows the terms. The distrust can be felt in the currency itself, which seems psychologically designed for people not to notice it at all. Money in most countries *feels* good. Dollars feel good. English fivers feel fine. Swiss bills make money feel like a joy in themselves, as though possession alone were synonymous with happiness. West German marks are harsh and tough and give a feeling of security.

Rubles don't feel like money at all. They are little more than half the size of dollar bills, of indeterminate paper, inducing no confidence in the touch. They seem to disappear into the wallet as though embarrassed to be seen, and are picked out between finger and thumb as though they were something not quite proper. They are illustrated with pictures of Lenin or sheaves of wheat and resemble tea coupons or, at best, play money for some Soviet version of Monopoly.

Somewhere the barriers between the Russians and the rest of the human race to which they have contributed so enormously had to be penetrated; somewhere the other barriers formed by Soviet trading practices which barred private commerce must be leaped. Jan Rokotov proved to be the man to do it, and he did it with singular brilliance.

The trial record said that he began as a one-man operation, then hired henchmen (thus breaking more laws) and finally formed a syndicate which, at its height, spread throughout the Soviet Union. Rokotov's runners waited all day outside the National, the Metropole, the Ukraine, the Peking, the Sovietskaya. They pestered tourists for their clothes, indifferent to size, age or origin, paying twice and three times what the clothes originally cost.

If the visitors showed no interest in rubles, Rokotov was able to pay them in portable antiques, like icons and genuinely old ornamented jewel boxes, which are almost unobtainable in the stores. These he bought personally in rural districts where old people still had a few possessions from before the Revolution of 1917. Or else he paid the tourists in Russian stamp collections (one of the few items, along with portraits of Lenin, in constantly abundant supply). Caviar and vodka he could also supply, cheaper than in the stores.

A pretty girl once asked me whether I knew any women in the Western embassies from whom she could buy dresses. "I don't mind how much I pay," she said wistfully, and the memory of her words always makes me sad, because I could not help. She would willingly have given $200 in rubles for a simple dress from Macy's or Gimbels.

I wondered at the time how a secretary earning perhaps $125 a month could afford such a huge sum, but Jan Rokotov knew. The girl lived either with her parents and grandparents in a small apartment or in a dormitory with other girls. Her meals at an office cafeteria would cost her only a few kopeks. Nothing in the stores was worth buying. Her money accumulated, and there was almost nothing to spend it on. Such people made up Rokotov's clientele.

But there were even better clients. This was a period of Russian economic expansion abroad. Russian businessmen were traveling to Africa, Asia and Latin America. Their allowance of foreign currency was humiliatingly small. It compelled them to live in embassy compounds or third-rate hotels, and put them at a tremendous psychological disadvantage to the free-spending Americans, the stylish Italians and the shrewd Japanese. Rokotov could supply them with all the currency they wanted, at a rate they were more than happy to pay. If they wanted, he could also fit them out more smartly.

Rokotov, it goes without saying, could also supply girls. The sex problem in Moscow is a difficult one indeed for inflamed travelers (although, heaven knows, there is little to inflame them either in the magazines or the movies). At every Intourist hotel, a formidable lady sits at a desk on each floor, at the head of the stairs and outside the elevators. Not the least of her duties is to keep an extremely careful lookout for any conduct she suspects may fall short of her own high moral standards. She also moonlights by spying for the K.G.B. on the side A tough obstacle to cross.

But there seemed to be no limit to Rokotov's inventiveness. If a tourist wanted a girl, Rakotov disguised her in thick glasses and a clerical pinafore, pulled her hair back in a puritanical bun and equipped her with a stenographic pad and pencil which she carried very conspicuously past the suspicious dragon at the floor desk. Once in the client's room the young lady presumably let her hair down, as it were.

In his first year of corporate management Jan Rokotov—and this is in the official court trial record, published in *Pravda*—grossed *half a million dollars*. The diversity of his contacts throughout the length and breadth of the Soviet Union was breathtaking. In his employ, paid in cash or goods, were pilots and stewardesses of Aeroflot, the Russian airline; Russian businessmen traveling abroad on official missions; interpreters and travel guides; Soviet Army officers on leave from occupied Eastern Europe, and even the stern and apparently incorruptible women of Intourist. And always he was the contact with tourists from the United States and Western Europe, easy to locate and always available.

Moscow is a city of seemingly unbreachable anonymity, with only a handful of public telephone directories, and nobody knows anybody. And yet Jan Rokotov was certainly known to hundreds of people in the Soviet nether world that exists between legality and crime. He actually became a trend-setter for younger Muscovites, to the extent that his influence spread to thousands of youngsters who had never heard his name. He is reported to have begun the fad of going hatless through the winter, an affectation that became almost synonymous in the Puritanical columns of the *Komsomolskaya Gazette*, with juvenile delinquency and "hooliganism." He introduced a taste for the narrow, cuffless trousers and pointed shoes favored by Italian dandies of the period.

It almost goes without saying that he maintained an unusually beautiful mistress, one Nadezhda Edlitsa. Nadezhda happened to have a husband, but for Rokotov that was a mere morsel. He shaved the fellow's horns by giving him a job in the organization.

But when the organization is formed and the profits are rolling in, there comes the crucial matter of what one can do with all that money in a drab society like the Soviet Union. The government issues every man and woman an internal passport, directs a man where he must live, how many square feet of space he is allowed to occupy, where and when he is permitted to take a holiday. It is a city of vouchers, form-filling, passes and receipts. Almost nothing can be done without written permission.

Because of the paucity of housing accommodation and things to buy, the Muscovite, even when he rises high in the scientific, artistic or literary professions, lives modestly—there is no alternative. Movie and ballet stars traveling in the West surprise their Western colleagues by the poor design and quality of their clothes. At the Cannes Film Festival the members of the Russian delegation look as though they had been misdirected from Coney Island. This helps to explain why Nureyev, Makarova and Baryshnikov, who arrived in the West as dowdy as the rest, turned overnight into peacocks. They wanted to buy up *everything*.

The slightest indication of conspicuous spending by a Muscovite citizen, especially by a man like Rokotov, who had no apparent job, would be observed instantly by the police, and his case investigated with great care.

Such a man—officially known in the Soviet Union as a parasite—would not be allowed to move into an apartment in any of the fashionable areas of the city, like Gorky Street or the Kutuzovsky Prospect or Lenin Prospect or Sadovaya Samchestnaya. The waiting list for a car is a matter of years and payment has to be in cash. Even then, questions would be asked as to why he wanted it, and how come he had the ready money to pay for it.

Vacations in the Black Sea resorts of Yalta and Sochi are usually limited to special factory groups, or privileged members of the Communist Party, or workers selected by the trade unions. A shiftless Russian without a job who turned up on the Black Sea in a car with his girl friend would be subject to immediate arrest. In every sphere of Soviet society, from birth to death and from breakfast until bedtime, the authorities have a legal mechanism which can forbid you to do it. And they are usually possessed of ample enthusiasm for enforcement.

Rokotov had the answer to all these problems. He had his men hired to wait in the office of the state lottery. He would discover the name and address of the holder of the winning ticket before it was officially announced and hurry to the winner's home. If the ticket was worth $30,000, Rokotov offered him $50,000 and bought it. He then had a legal excuse for free spending. For a new car he would approach a man who had strained his way through the waiting list and buy it, at double the price. His holidays in Sochi were covered by the lottery tickets, as were the restaurant checks at the Aragvy, Ararat and Budapest, the three best restaurants in the city.

There remained the problem of an apartment. Being the son of working-class parents and describing himself only as a clerk, he was entitled to little more than the corner of a crowded room. He needed entree into the society of those Muscovites entitled to "privileged accommodation" (which usually means a two-room apartment, with rooms the size of large closets). So he appointed as his chief lieutenant one Vladislav Faibishenko, a young playboy in his twenties whose parents were simply described in the court testimony as "well-to-do." They had a large apartment and a dacha in the country. Faibishenko persuaded his parents to spend most of their time in the fresh air of the country, while Rokotov and Nadezhda moved into the apartment.

His social arrangements were now complete. His itinerary as officially recorded resembled that of some self-made business mogul, which he most certainly was. He rarely rose before three in the afternoon. He had the latest American jazz records—this was some years before the abundance of tapes and cassettes. His green Volga car, then the least dreary of Russian automobiles, made a nightly pilgrimage up and down Gorky Street, which

Rokotov preferred to call "Broad-vay," a habit which has remained with young Muscovites to this day.

He made his office in expensive restaurants and hotel lobbies. He would sit at a table with Nadezhda and his cronies, enjoying the dubious pleasures of the Russian cuisine. Agents came and went as he ate, some having flown from distant parts of the country. Coded telegrams were delivered to his table. He would get up a score of times in the evening to make telephone calls—all his business was done on pay phones. After dinner selected guests were invited to the Faibishenko apartment for "wild orgies."

The reverberation of the new Russian image Rokotov set up even had its own backlash—similar to the backlash of the "silent majority" and the "hard hats." Its chief participants were the youngsters and teachers of the Komsomol, the fanatic Communist youth organization.

Stalin was only eight years dead, four years discredited. When the Komsomol leaders, young men and girls in their late teens and early twenties, learned of Khrushchev's denunciation they reacted with a horror that could scarcely be exaggerated. They obediently denounced the "cult of personality," but in their hearts they pined for Stalin's avuncular tyranny, which gave them the luxury of spying and eavesdropping on their neighbors. They hated the new freedom, because it compelled them to think thoughts they would have preferred to ignore.

The *stilyagy*, as they were called—a term that had disappeared from contemporary Gorky Street slang as "teddy boy" and "spiv" have disappeared from British slang—offered the young Puritans the chance they subconsciously sought for vengeance against the new, hated permissiveness. Cases were reported where Komsomol militants seized the kids and slit the seams of their narrow trousers. In addition to the castration symbol of such an act, there were also interesting examples of rape and incest symbols. Girls were publicly seized and the lipstick wiped off their mouth—not so drastic as the French shaving the heads of girls who slept with Germans, but the game was the same. Old-line Stalinist fathers bent their daughters' heads over the basin and scrubbed their faces. All this was written up with approval in the Moscow press.

The establishment hatred against Jan Rokotov was not dissimilar to that which built up about four years later in England against the doctor-playboy Stephen Ward in the Profumo scandal. The predominant emotion was really envy. Ward's crime was in getting away with what he should not have done within the conventions of established society. As with Stephen Ward in 1963, Rokotov walked a tightrope, and it was clear in retrospect that the first stumble would spell his destruction. He survived for four and a half years, during which time he grossed several million dollars. He was so successful that he graduated to a belief in his own invulnerability, and in the rule followed by the American robber barons of the nineteenth century: that money can buy anything, and every man has his price.

It is a precept that tends to be fatal in the end, as history has proved from Boss Tweed to vanishing Boss Hoffa. In Rokotov's case, trouble came from the last quarter he expected. Edlits, the husband of Nadezhda, considered himself entitled to more money. Rokotov, aware that Edlits was doing very well indeed, believed he was bluffing and told him to go away. Edlits did go away—and informed the police. The date was February 23, 1961, and the luck of the King of the League of Lucky Gentlemen had finally run out.

Rokotov's apartment was raided by scores of policemen, and an incredible cache was found: millions of dollars in a dozen currencies. The dumbfounded forces of the law next raided Nadezhda's home and found $700,000 more in cash. She had not even bothered to hide the money, but kept it in drawers and boxes.

The trial was held behind closed doors a few months later, in

July. Rokotov, Faibishenko, Nadezhda Edlitsa, her husband and five others were the principal defendants. The Western press was barred and depended on leaks from spectators who had been admitted to the courtroom and on the official reports, which were published in *Pravda* and *Izvestia*.

The papers reported it as a morality tale. They described Rokotov and his henchmen as wallowing in a sink of filth and degradation. They compared the scenes of the orgies and the jazz fests to the serene, dedicated lives of Soviet youths who were far too happy serving the cause of Communism to waste thoughts on silly stuff like wads and wads of money and scores of pretty girls. It is not inconceivable, however, that *some* readers of these accounts, in faraway places like Krasnoyarsk, Magnitogorsk and Chelyabinsk, may have had a fleeting, if unworthy, wish that some of the filth and degradation had rubbed off on them, even as envy of Stephen Ward was felt as far afield as Wigan and Rochdale.

The trial was conducted according to Soviet protocol. Everybody pleaded guilty and expressed remorse at the awful things he had done. If *Pravda* is to be believed—which it isn't— Jan Rokotov said, "I have thought my life over. It was an ugly life, useless to myself and to everybody else. I have never had any peace of mind. I always had to go on making money. I could not stop. I am very sorry about this, and I rely on the humanity and compassion of our People's Courts."

He had to be joking!

It is difficult to imagine a more dubious humanity on which to rely, unless perhaps it may be one of Idi Amin's military tribunals in Uganda. Rokotov was sentenced to twenty years in jail. Faibishenko and Nadezhda drew fifteen years each. Edlits, Nadezhda's husband, was freed without sentence, doubtless for turning state's evidence against his wife and his benefactor.

But now we come to what Robert Browning would call the twist in the wrist of the story. A week or two later the Supreme Court of the Soviet Union decided to reintroduce capital punishment by decree. Although Rokotov and his unlucky gentlemen had already been sentenced and were serving their sentences, it seemed a good idea to the public prosecutor to try the new decree out on them, presumably to see how it worked. The prosecutor appealed to the People's Courts against the prison sentences, asking for the death penalty instead. The court agreed, and on July 27, 1961, both Rokotov and Faibishenko fell before a firing squad.

In this manner the Soviet Union deprived itself of the services of a man who might have enriched a society less enmeshed in the nineteenth-century Marxian ethic, which experience has shown simply does not work. In the final accounting Rokotov's enterprise and energy contributed several millions of dollars and other hard currency to enrich the Soviet economy. If he had not been denounced he might be contributing even more millions today.

The sentences were presumably intended as a grim warning to other bright young Russians who might be interested in making a dishonest buck. I wondered, while I was reading the news reports, whether the warning would be properly effective. I was not in Moscow at the time of the Rokotov revelations and ate up the story in the newspapers. When I did return some months later, it was with a question in my mind.

I left the Metropole Hotel on a fine cold day for a stroll through Sverdlovsk Square. I was bareheaded, and recall well that I was wearing a Prince of Wales checked suit made by Tony Sinclair of Conduit Street, Mayfair, and a red cashmere pullover. I had not even reached the edge of the pavement to cross the square when a gaunt, gray-faced young man detached himself from the moving mass of humanity, which in Moscow never seems to be going anywhere.

"Sir," he said softly, walking by my side and touching my elbow.

"*Ne panimayu*," I said. "I do not understand."

"American?"

"No."

"*Deutsch?*"

"*Nein.*"

"*Français?*"

"*Non.*"

He gave up on nationality and continued, smattering in a mixture of English and German. "Do you have anything to sell? Shoes? Suits? Chewing gum? Blue jeans? Razor blades? Are you with your wife? Would she sell her nylons? Dresses? Anything you want to sell, I will give you a good price. At a ruble to the dollar. A very good price indeed."

I laughed. My question was answered, and I relented a little. In Moscow it is always a good idea to keep a few items in one's pockets for people who amuse and so deserve reward. I gave him a pack of Wrigley's chewing gum. To his credit, he immediately thrust a hand into his pocket to pay for it, but I waved him away and we parted friends.

Since the sad demise of Jan Rokotov the Soviet newspapers periodically burst into ever-more-angry exposés of capitalist practices. There have been stories of a Moscow syndicate which employed—without payment—mental patients in a therapy ward to make knitted goods for the black market; of a clandestine lipstick factory which grossed more than a million dollars; of a team of wool thieves who commuted back and forth between Moscow and Vladivostok—about as far in the Soviet Union as one can travel.

The authorities not too long ago made public the all but unbelievable story of an Odessa man in his seventies who had been conducting a flourishing trade in gold, gems and currency of many denominations ever since the Bolshevik Revolution of 1917! One diamond found in his home was estimated to be worth $100,000. Other stones he had hidden in the stove, in tin cans and, best of all, in the urns which he kept on the graves of his grandmother, his mother, and his wife.

More recently, scandals in real estate finagling have been

leveled at the late Madame Furtseva, the former Minister of Culture, and also at the governor of the notoriously corrupt Georgia. Of this one can be sure: If someone of Furtseva's stature was doing it, they are all doing it, and are either not getting found out or *are* getting found out, and distributing the payola.

Today the black market is rife. Men accost the visitor in the street with offers like, "Hey, buddy, I give you three rubles to the dollar" (the current official exchange rate is eighty-five cents to the ruble). The police, although they are legally obliged to prosecute and the courts to apply the death penalty, are looking the other way, clearly on orders of the K.G.B. If my last visit is to be any yardstick, Moscow during the Olympics in 1980 will be open house for any kind of illegal exchange whatever: money, clothes, watches, whatever the Westerner possesses, on his back or in his hotel room.

It will be interesting to see what the impact will be, on Moscow society in general and the old Stalinist moralists in particular. There might even be another revolution. The King is dead, but his loyal subjects are alive and doing very well in Moscow.

6

A Rendezvous in Sverdlovsk Square

"Moscow is my least favorite city. I would never go there if I wanted to have fun."

—Edwin Newman

I left the Bolshoi Theater after a performance of *Eugene Onegin* into a snowstorm that felt like frozen iron filings. The crowds hustled toward the Metro or cried in vain for taxis. I had in mind to take the underpass under Sverdlovsk, enter the Metropole Hotel and have a warming drink at the cocktail bar. The performance had been stupendous, and I needed to sit alone and savor it. The walk to my hotel, the National, short though it was, was too daunting in the bitterly cold darkness.

I had almost reached the underpass when a girl took my arm. She was wrapped in fur and was quite agreeable to look at, except that the cold had turned her cheeks, like those of everybody else in Moscow, a kind of dark, chapped purple. Her eyes were shy and alarmed. She spoke rapidly, nervously, in German, without questioning whether or not I understood the language.

"I am sorry to bother you, but could you buy me some cigarettes, please?"

(I should belatedly say that German is the lingua franca throughout Eastern Europe, and almost all conversations recorded in this book were in German.)

This was not quite the kind of panhandling I was used to in Moscow. I replied, "*Natürlich*. I don't smoke myself, but we can buy some."

This was the beginning of a curious encounter, my introduction into the kind of privileged life that is not supposed to exist in the Soviet Union, but which, as I indicated in a previous chapter, most certainly does. Few outsiders get to witness it, so in a small way I suppose I won quite a scoop from the Western community.

The girl said, "Where?"

I said, "Come with me. We will go and buy some at the bar of the Metropole Hotel. But let's get on with it, Fräulein, because I am freezing to death here. My clothes are not as warm as yours."

The girl's teeth too were beginning to chatter, but she did not move.

"Wait," she said. "You must wait here. It is very important."

"Wait for what?"

The girl (I will call her Ilena from now on) looked even more nervous. She stammered, "No ... wait ... you must first meet my good friend, Ludmilla, who is waiting inside the Bolshoi."

She took my hand and led me back to the Bolshoi, which was still discharging its bundled-up horde of ballet-lovers.

"Wait for me," she said again, and disappeared.

"Hurry up," I called after her. "It's freezing, and I want to go home."

Five minutes seemed like an hour in the subzero cold. I owned no heavy clothes, and I could feel the dirty sheet ice of the pavement seeping through my thin Italian soles and freezing my toes. I had turned to leave when Ilena returned, pulling along her girl friend.

Ludmilla—that is not her name either—was, from the neck up

at any rate, stunningly beautiful. Her blond hair was dressed in Teutonic plaits, and her slanting, lime-green Tartar eyes were enhanced, not too expertly, with eyeliner—not then available in Moscow, nor is it, I believe, today. In the beam Ludmilla was somewhat broad, like many Russian girls. What was immediately noticeable, however, was her heavy mink coat. Ludmilla was a very elegant young lady indeed. I estimated them both to be in their early twenties, although the climate tends to make Russian girls look older than they are.

Through chattering teeth I invited them both across to the Metropole for a warming drink. "I will come with you," Ludmilla said imperiously. "Ilena will stay here, look for a taxi and wait for us until we finish."

"Isn't that a bit hard on poor Ilena?" I asked. Ilena, in fact, was turning blue.

"Ilena doesn't mind, do you, Ilena?"

"No," said Ilena, in a voice which suggested she dared not say otherwise.

I interfered no further and escorted Ludmilla through the underpass to the Metropole. In the bar I ordered a brandy for myself. Ludmilla said, "Gin and tonic, please."

I made a mental note of what was considered chic in the Moscow younger set. Clearly gin was in, and vodka was not *kulturny*. But I had not seen anything yet. I asked what kind of cigarettes she wanted, and she asked for Kents. I bought her a couple of cartons. Ludmilla drank her gin and tonic quickly. She was clearly in a hurry to go and drummed her fingers impatiently as I lingered over my brandy.

Outside, poor Ilena, bluer than ever, was fighting off people trying to steal her taxi. I opened the door for them, assuming that with the purchase of the American cigarettes my usefulness to them was at an end. It had been an interesting confrontation and had put me in good humor for my return to my hotel.

"Auf Wiedersehen," I said.

Both girls looked at me in alarm, looked back at each other, then back at me, even more alarmed. Ludmilla clutched Ilena's forearm, and the driver watched us all with complete disinterest, waiting for his instructions.

"*Nicht auf Wiedersehen,*" they both said almost simultaneously. "You must come along with us immediately, or we will lose the taxi."

"Where?"

"Home."

It was only because I was suddenly wary that I repeated the question. Again they replied together, and with increasing urgency, "*Nach heimat.*"

I thought it over quickly as I grew colder, the steam from my breath growing thicker, the water from my eyes turning into pearls as I blinked, the Bolshoi crowds shoving. It would be impossible to find oneself in Moscow in a situation against which one is more specifically warned by the resident Western community. But it seemed to me that the chance was simply not one to be missed. I got into the back seat beside Ludmilla. Ilena sat in the front seat next to the cloth-capped, earmuffed taxi driver.

The taxi seemed to travel for miles, past block after block of gray apartment buildings, identical, doorless (most Moscow apartment buildings have their main entrance at the back; the front is reserved for the community's shops). I kept looking out of the frozen windows to establish some sort of direction, but I had long since lost my bearings and could see only that we were going roughly north.

Ilena saw my straining eyes. "*Angst?*" she asked, rather sardonically.

"I'm not worried at all," I said, nettled. "Just trying to get my bearings."

But I noticed that Ludmilla frequently looked through the rear window, from what I could only conclude was nervousness at the idea of being followed. I decided that they belonged to one of three categories. They wanted to change their rubles for hard currency, so that they could make purchases at the Berioska shops. Or they were K.G.B. agents interested in involving a "German" foreign correspondent in a compromising situation; my very imperfect and rusty German was, at least, better than theirs. Or else they were hookers, in which case one would presume Ludmilla would show some sign of professional affection. This she emphatically did not.

One of the things that fascinated me about the two girls was their relationship, and Ludmilla's flagrantly dominating attitude. I could just imagine the scene in the front lobby of the Bolshoi that preceded our meeting: the two standing looking for Westerners; seeing someone (me) idiotic enough to be wearing a spring overcoat and Italian loafers in Moscow in midwinter; Ludmilla saying, "Get *him*," but staying prudently in the warmth while Ilena trotted after me in the snow.

It was past midnight when we arrived at a modern apartment block in the nondescript style that blankets Moscow's suburbs in ineffable dreariness. Even for luxury apartments the Russians see no need to waste money on lobby display, so one always feels one is using the tradesmen's entrance. We climbed three flights and Ludmilla let us into her flat. The foyer was the size of a large closet; nevertheless it contained clothes racks, book-shelves and a large refrigerator. "My grandmother is asleep in the next room," Ludmilla whispered.

We went into Ludmilla's room, which was of standard Soviet postwar design: small, cramped, too long for the width, defying tasteful decoration. But it was crammed with the latest equipment. There were a large TV set, a hi-fi, tape recorder and two transistors. On the walls were autographed photographs of opera singers.

I helped the girls off with their heavy coats. One of the suffocating factors of living in Moscow is the sheer space taken up by winter clothes. They have to be hung everywhere and give any room the feeling of being in a padded cell, a feeling intensified by the double windows needed to keep out the cold.

Ilena wore a light flowered frock and a sagging cardigan in some kind of synthetic material. Ludmilla wore a smart blue suit of Western cut, but badly rumpled as though she wore it in her sleep. Thawing out, all three of us sniffled and blew noses loudly. The atmosphere was anything but romantic.

"How do you like this suit I am wearing?" Ludmilla demanded.

"Charming," I said.

"I bought it at the Berioska shop in the Metropole last year."

"Splendid."

Ludmilla then opened the refrigerator and took out a bottle of sweet champagne. From the next room an old woman's voice was querulously raised in what sounded like a complaint at the noise we were making. Ludmilla popped the cork and replied something to the effect of, "Shut up, and go back to sleep." Through the thin dividing wall could be heard mumbling.

We sat down on the two chairs and on Ludmilla's red-covered divan-bed and drank toasts to ourselves, to the Bolshoi and to the joys of shopping in Berioska stores. Ilena played tapes of "Strangers in the Night," then "Lara's Theme" from *Dr. Zhivago.*

Ludmilla opened her handbag, put one of her new cigarettes in her mouth and snapped her fingers at Ilena. Ilena reached into her own bag and lit the cigarette with a lighter. Ludmilla took a photograph album from a shelf and leafed through the pages with me. Her father was a handsome man with dark, wavy hair and a beaky, somewhat saturnine profile. The photos showed him wearing casual sports clothes, but also a dinner jacket and once even white tie and tails. Ludmilla's mother was also good-looking. One photograph showed father, mother and daughter celebrating some occasion in what appeared to be a good restaurant.

"A very handsome family," I said, and to my dismay Ludmilla's eyes filled with huge tears.

"Ludmilla's mother and father were both killed last year," Ilena said quietly. "In a car crash. It was very tragic, and Ludmilla has not yet recovered."

"I'm sorry."

All sorts of confused un-Sovietlike impressions were trying to form themselves into a coherent whole in my mind. Heavy mink, hi-fi, white tie and tails ... and now that supremely capitalist form of mortality. Ilena seemed to read my thoughts.

"Ludmilla's father was an orchestra conductor," she said. "He was very rich."

Ludmilla set her sadness aside and got down to business. It was predictable: her rubles for my dollars. I had no objection. I had been changing my traveler's checks at the hotel, where they disappeared into the ever-open maw of the Soviet exchequer. I saw no reason why Ludmilla and Ilena should not reap the benefit, even if it were illegal.

"Sure," I said. "What would you like? Fifty dollars? A hundred?"

"What you will," said Ludmilla. "Look."

She opened the top drawer of a gimcrack chest of drawers, and the contents were so startling I could scarcely believe it as I record it now. The drawer was full of *money*. Fifty- and hundred-ruble bills in wads. There must have been at least four thousand dollars' worth! My grandiloquent offer of a hundred made me feel like an ass.

"You are quite a capitalist," I said inadequately.

"Ludmilla's father left her a lot," Ilena explained.

Ludmilla was not yet finished with me. Her slanting eyes gleaming with triumph and acquisitiveness, she slammed the drawer shut and opened the next. It was packed with French perfume. Schiaperelli, Guerlain, Cardin, Chanel—the biggest collection I had ever seen in the possession of anyone, in or out of France. It also occurred to me, had I ever seen four thousand dollars in cash before in my life? Anywhere? Except perhaps peering into my bank teller's open till. Well, now I was seeing it, in a cramped, surburban apartment in the capital of world Communism.

So I gave Ludmilla a hundred dollars, and she gave me a hundred rubles. I protested that it was too much, that the rate was then only eighty-five cents to the ruble, but she waved the protests aside. Russians, I have found, are either grasping to the last kopek (in the catering trades) or completely slapdash about money values.

Business done, we drank champagne and danced a little. I confess to making a mild pass at Ludmilla, not that I had the slightest carnal desire, but merely with journalistic curiosity as to her reaction. There was no reaction. She neither pushed my hand away, nor did she give the slightest sign of encouragement. She was a big girl, of course—perhaps she hadn't noticed.

I asked if the two girls lived together. "No," said Ilena, "but when it gets late, Ludmilla lets me stay here." They informed me they were students of journalism at Moscow University. The university is on the other side of the city from the apartment. I asked if they traveled by bus or by the Metro. I could have kicked myself for sounding so lower-class when Ludmilla coolly answered, "I always take a taxi. It comes to the door and picks me up."

She then asked, "Which of us is prettier, Ilena or me?" I was glad of the question; by now I was tired of playing straight man to the haughty Ludmilla. "Ilena," I said without hesitation, and to drive my point home I winked at her. The gentle Ilena looked startled at such *lèse majesté*. Ludmilla growled something Russian under her breath, picked up a pale-blue telephone and called a taxi for me.

She accompanied me downstairs, leaving Ilena presumably trembling at the anger which would be vented on her. She noticed I did not smoke and gave me a cigarette from her pack. "Give it to the driver as a tip," she said. "He'll understand." She gave me a conspiratorial grin as though I knew what she was talking about, which I didn't.

Despite warnings from Western friends I continued to see the two girls, and they introduced me to various university friends, both boys and girls, the *jeunesse dorée* so assiduously serviced by Jan Rokotov less than a decade before. I heard one friend of Ludmilla's complaining, in the languid accent one usually associates with girls named Lady Jane This, or the Honorable Penelope That: "I'm so furious," she said, making a *moue*, "that Daddy insisted on selling his car after Ludmilla's parents died. Now we have to go out to our dacha every weekend in the electric train. Such a bore."

And another girl, who told me she came from Petersburg (*"not* Leningrad" she emphasized), made remarks about the African exchange students at the university that would have gratified the Ku Klux Klan. Nor did the others argue the subject with her.

I was haunted by shades of Jan Rokotov. Newspaper headlines were coming to life before my eyes—to such an extent that I could see my adventure someday written in *Izvestia*'s (happily) inimitable style:

"Ludmilla Petrovna K. . . . has been ordered by the Soviet bench of justices to leave Moscow and not return for five years. She has been dismissed from Moscow University. This wretched student disgraced the U.S.S.R. and the noble memory of a distinguished father by involving herself in illegal and disgusting transactions, made ardent by the ceaseless flow of champagne in her grandmother's apartment, with a Western correspondent so decadent he thinks it is clever to wear Italian shoes in Moscow, the coldest January since the Battle of the Volga. The girl confessed, pleaded guilty, admitted that she had led a useless life, and begged for the forgiveness of the People's Courts. . . ."

The awful thing about all this is that it would be extremely hard to deny any of it!

7

Moscow's Swinging Spies

The trouble with walking in Moscow is that the avenues and squares are so huge, the further you walk the further away you seem to be from where you are trying to get.

—ANTHONY DELANO, London *Daily Mirror*

Although presidents like Nixon, royals like Prince Philip and *le beau monde* on principle detest the media, a fling at journalism has often been enjoyed by bluebloods. Three generations of Churchill—Sir Winston, Randolph and young Winston—have all been practicing journalists. Lord Snowdon works today for the London *Sunday Times*. Jacqueline Onassis, Lynda Bird Johnson, Sargent Shriver, and David Eisenhower are four Americans of high political lineage who have worked for the press.

But when one discovers the identical phenomenon in Moscow, one raises one's eyebrows and one asks, why? Because everything in Russia is so unlike what it is in the west, the similarities rather than the contradictions are what stick in the mind, like corn kernels in the teeth.

Anatoly Andreyevich Gromyko, the son of the eternal Soviet Foreign Minister, abandoned a featherbed diplomatic career about eight years ago to become a department head at the Novosti Press Agency in Moscow, and also to write an appalling book about the United States. Galina Brezhnev, daughter of

Brezhnev himself, worked until recently in the same agency. So, I believe, does Julia Petrova, Khrushchev's granddaughter.

Why Novosti? And what is Novosti anyway? Novosti (Russian for gossiplike news) is a news, feature and picture agency housed in a modern, glass-fronted building on Pushkin Square. It is one of the most un-Russian institutions in Russia.

At Novosti pretty secretaries in modified miniskirts answer the telephones. Copies of American and French magazines lie around on the desks. Writers and photographers run around looking busy and harassed. When you hand in your calling card, whoever you want to meet sends his secretary or comes himself. There are no "*nyets*," no "impossibles" uttered by disembodied voices behind opaque windows, no lines like "The person you wish to speak to is out of the city, and we don't know when he will be back"—phrases with which Soviet officials traditionally protect themselves against Western correspondents.

Novosti has contacts with the giant press associations, newspapers and magazines of the West. It produces *Soviet Life* magazine, and also the highly professional, abysmally dull *Sputnik*, the Russian overt imitation of *Reader's Digest*. Novosti is rightly pleased with its own sophistication. "We are commercial," the editors like to tell you. "We are nongovernmental. We have to make a profit." After which the senior editors, at any rate, leap into their cars and speed off for long weekends at their dachas.

What they do *not* say, however, and are very pained when others say it, is the fact that Novosti is the brainchild of the K.G.B., the Russian secret police.

K.G.B. (*Komityet Gosudarstvennoy Besapasnosti*, or State Security Agency) is the successor to Cheka, O.G.P.U. and N.K.V.D. It still operates in the darker corners of life, with its huge espionage apparatus, its hounding of intellectuals and dissenters, and its silent war against the United States and Britain. But in Russia today few people worry any more about the doorbell ringing at three in the morning, and the research and analysis side of the K.G.B. actually has lighter, more constructive functions. Like the C.I.A. and the British S.I.S., it attracts some of the brightest young men from the universities— the Russian equivalent of Ivy Leaguers, the best linguists, philosophers and writers. They join the K.G.B. after rigorous examination and enjoy high pay, shopping privileges, intellectual stimulation, promotion and foreign travel to exotic places. In many ways it is one of the most cultured and tolerant organizations in the Soviet Union.

One of the most important tasks for these young men is to seek to understand what makes the West tick. By that I don't mean what makes American nuclear bombs tick; they know all about that themselves. They seek the unfathomables of Western society, such as what on earth Americans see in American football; why so many Commonwealth countries are obsessed by cricket; why Americans chew gum, eat with their forks in their right hand instead of their left and daub their subway trains with graffiti.

France interests the K.G.B. much less. French culture dominated tsarist Russia for so many centuries that they feel they know the French very well, down to the rudeness that unites Muscovites and Parisians, a theme repeated endlessly, but inevitably, in this book.

Toward the end of the 1950s, senior officers at the K.G.B. headquarters on Dzerzhinsky Street began a serious inquiry into Western journalism. They wondered why glossy magazines like *Playboy*, *McCall's*, *Town & Country*, *Elle*, *Paris-Match*, and serious publications like *Harper's* and *L'Express*, flood the world, and would flood the Soviet Union if they were not so rigorously banned. Why did Western wire services, like A.P., U.P.I., Reuters, and Agence France-Presse, enjoy worldwide prestige while Tass, in its own way a very muscular and efficient organization, with top-class, discerning correspondents, has almost no influence outside the U.S.S.R. Why do Soviet diplomats at the United Nations and in Washington read *The*

New York Times before *Pravda* if they think no one is looking. Why has the B.B.C. World Service, broadcasting only 750 hours a week, far more listeners than Moscow Radio, which broadcasts more than three thousand hours to the free world?

K.G.B. seniors then assembled the Institute of Journalists and one or two International Friendship and Knowledge Groups. In February 1961 the combined brains formed the Novosti Press Agency as an editorial service that would not only resemble a Western agency in style and operation, but would also instill into its editors, writers, photographers, and even into its secretaries and librarians, something of the same sense of collective morale and loyalty as, say, *Paris-Match*, the London *Daily Mirror* and magazines like *Time* and *Newsweek*.

For a society as suspicious and bureaucratic as that of the Soviet Union, it was a revolutionary and even frightening concept. In matters like atom bombs and space programs they'll take *anything* from the West—buy it, spy on it, steal it. But to take the techniques of the media was something else altogether. If Russian journalists were allowed to investigate, they would also have to think for themselves. Still, the project went ahead.

Not only did the fledgling Novosti enjoy the service of K.G.B. whizz kids who spoke English like Americans, but it had a more than useful kernel of Western defectors who were professional journalists by experience, even though a little rusty.

Guy Burgess had been a journalist. Ralph Parker, an Englishman and wearer of some old school tie or other, had made the bizarre transition from the Moscow bureau of the London *Times* to the Moscow bureau of the *Daily Worker*. Novosti also had the good fortune to tap the talents of a first-rate foreign correspondent in Wilfred Burchett, the Australian who covered the Korean War from the North Korean side and the Vietnam War from Hanoi for the Communist *Humanité* of Paris. Burchett had once been a correspondent for the London *Daily Express*. (In 1973, back in Australia, he sued an Australian parliamentarian who had accused him of treason. After a long, sensational trial, in which former prisoners of the North Koreans were paraded, Burchett lost.)

Another couple of eccentrics available to the agency were Archibald Johnstone and Robert Dalgleish. They were both editors of *British Ally*, a magazine published in Moscow in the heyday of Anglo-Soviet relations. When Stalin closed the magazine down they tore up their British passports and became Soviet citizens. (I will try to explain elsewhere the intriguing reason why so many defectors went east during the most withering period of the Cold War: Burgess, Maclean, Johnstone, Dalgleish, and the American Noel Field and his family, who escaped to the Hungary of the diabolical Rakosi.)

The ever-mysterious Victor Louis was also a journalist-*cum*-K.G.B. man. A Russian, married to an English girl, the former Jennifer Statham, Louis was available. For years now he has walked a political tightrope that has dazzled and baffled Moscow correspondents. He has a foot in both camps, and whenever you read a Moscow dispatch which begins, "Informed sources state . . ." what they really mean is, "Victor Louis told me. . . ."

In founding Novosti money was no object. One editor told me, when the agency was still young, "We always have lots of dough." A four-story building, glass-windowed at street level, was built, and it contains all the latest equipment for transmitting news and pictures. It could be a Western wire agency but for the somewhat pervasive evidence of the lavatories; Russians are not hot on drains.

A Council of Sponsors was formed. One founder-member was Aleksey Adzhubey, son-in-law of Khrushchev and then the nepotic editor of *Izvestia*. After a year of experimental work and dry runs, Novosti opened its foreign service and went into optimistic competition with Tass.

It had many teething troubles. Western publications which dealt with Novosti were often given static photographs and long-winded features more suitable for *Soviet Tractor Monthly*, if there is such a magazine. Sometimes its news was as much as four days behind Tass, whose dispatches it often merely rewrote.

But Novosti persevered. It sought outside advice—it even sought mine. I suggested, as an experienced magazine writer in both the United States and Britain, that I should travel around the Soviet Union, at Novosti's expense, and brighten up the dreary *Sputnik* with nonpolitical articles about the country, aimed squarely at American and British readership. They bought me chicken à la Kiev at the Aragvy Restaurant instead. "We are a digest," they chided gently. "Just like the *Reader's Digest*."

In 1963 Novosti acquired a major reinforcement when Kim Philby turned up rather hastily, a step ahead of arrest as a spy. Philby had the double advantage of being both a K.G.B. espionage agent and an eminently professional journalist. To mask his espionage activities he had been working in Beirut as correspondent for the London *Observer* and the London *Economist*. As always, wherever he moved, his personality galvanized the people around him, and his consumption of alcohol impressed even the Russians.

"Poor Philby," an American correspondent said to me in Moscow in late 1963, "former chief of intelligence in the British Foreign Office, former foreign correspondent for two of Britain's most distinguished publications—now he's exiled in Moscow working for a second-rate Soviet wire service."

But where all the other defectors had been in Moscow for years and had forgotten what life outside was like, Philby was fresh, had new ideas and succeeded admirably when he could be sufficiently sobered up. Today Novosti serves 640 Soviet newspapers and magazines and has correspondents in nearly eighty capitals, including three in Washington. Significantly, however, they do not have their own bureaus. They operate out of the embassies, and it has been estimated that more than half the staffs of the Soviet embassies in non-Communist countries work either for the K.G.B. or military intelligence. Almost half the ambassadors to non-Communist countries are K.G.B. and not Foreign Office employees.

Inevitably, Novosti foreign correspondents, being in large part intelligence agents, have burned their fingers and plunged the agency into serious international trouble. Britain, Brazil, Kenya and Zaire have all expelled correspondents at various times, or else warned them to stop meddling in domestic politics.

But the stumbles are more than compensated for by the sprints. Novosti's general prestige has given the K.G.B. confidence in its ability to communicate, to improve its standing, and even acquire some Ian Flemingesque glamour of its own.

When I was in Moscow in the mid-sixties a fictional series was running in eleven long installments in *Komsomolskaya Pravda*, the youth magazine, in which the heroine was a glamorous and intrepid K.G.B. girl. Her name was Natasha, and she dressed both correctly and with chic. Unlike her counterparts in the West, she loses no clothes in the course of her adventures. She contends with a Russian traitor who tries to smuggle nuclear secrets to the United States Embassy on the Ulitsa Chaikovskovo (how any Russian could hope to get through the Soviet police barrier at the American Embassy is not mentioned in the story). In the end, of course, Natasha gets her man.

In the same year, and shortly after I left Moscow, a film called "State Criminal" came out of Mosfilm Studios. The plot is rather complicated. The hero is a thoroughly decent K.G.B. agent, who dresses rather like Superman when Superman is pretending to be Clark Kent. When working behind his desk he unbuttons his collar and loosens his tie. He falls in love with a girl who happens to be the daughter of the traitor he is tracking down. There is a crisis of conscience, and the final twist is ingenious. She is not the man's daughter at all, only his foster daughter. This makes everything all right and leaves love free to triumph. The fact that foster parents and foster children can love each other did not apparently occur to anyone.

Since then the campaign to popularize the K.G.B. seems to have died away in the Russian media.

Novosti is undoubtedly the K.G.B.'s biggest public-relations success, and, in its own way, it also renders a great service to the West. It has proved an increasing boon to foreign correspondents. In pre-Novosti days there was almost no access to anybody or anything in Moscow. Telephone calls to officials were never returned, or else the official was never in. Today Novosti is positively eager to come to the correspondent's aid— at a price. ("We are commercial, old man. We have to make a profit, like you capitalists, ha! ha! ha!")

Need a photographer? Novosti will supply one—and also take a few pictures of you while you are not looking, for the files. Need a three-thousand-word feature on the holy city of Zagorsk? Novosti will supply you with one, written as reverently as all get out. Want to meet Maya Plissetskaya, the Bolshoi's *prima ballerina assoluta?* Novosti will set it up—but there is always a Novosti man or woman present.

That was how Novosti inadvertently gave George Feifer an extraordinary scoop some years ago. Plissetskaya—with Novosti hovering around—permitted Feifer to write a major profile about her. The Novosti contact man left them alone for only a matter of minutes while he went to the lavatory, and Plissetskaya revealed that she had been forced by authorities to add her name to a denunciation of Israel by Russian Jewish intellectuals. Had she refused to sign the petition, she said, there would be no more foreign tours for her.

Novosti does not always succeed. ("We are only human, you know.") Some years ago I asked the agency if I could interview Tatyana Samoilova, the gorgeous Russian star of *The Cranes Are Flying.* Miss Samoilova, by her beauty and by her tempestuous personality, made herself the first, and remains today the only, real Russian star in the Western sense of the word. Her success had been accompanied by the usual neuroses associated with film stars: nervous breakdowns, divorces, a reputation for indiscipline and unpunctuality.

"Nothing easier," said Novosti, forgetting for the moment that Samoilova is one of the few personalities in their artistic world who make their own rules. She told Novosti, and me, to get lost.

The year before Miss Samoilova had been given star billing, even within the Soviet Union, in a new superspectacular *Anna Karenina*. There was none of the usual "T. Samoilova" in small letters. Her name on the posters was almost as big as Tolstoy's. It proved to be a bomb, and to the best of my knowledge it has never been shown in the West. The Russians never publicize their artistic flops, any more than they publicize their air crashes or crime rates. *Anna Karenina* was presumably relegated to neighborhood theaters in Siberia, where the poor slobs are grateful for anything. I am quite certain that had *Anna Karenina* been a success, Miss Samoilova would have been graciously happy to receive me. As it was, she was certainly sulking.

I have followed Novosti's progress with interest and sympathy almost from its creation. The editors have always been of the greatest help to me. Its friendliness is unquestioned. Its staff has tried—and failed—to get Western journalists admitted as honorary members to the Moscow Journalists' Club—a very good club, incidentally, with an excellent restaurant and pleasant ambience, where members play chess through the night. It would be a superb irony if one ultimately had the K.G.B. to thank for bringing Soviet and Western correspondents together. They would continue to distrust each other profoundly—but what journalists don't?

That Novosti—and K.G.B.—operate under deep internal pressures, there is no doubt. *Sputnik* publishes the names of its editorial staff on its masthead, Western fashion. Over the years I have watched the names of my various professional friends there disappear, one by one. They were all charming, first-rate fellows, eager to help and full of all normal personal ambition.

One introduced me to his stunning mistress, whom he was assiduously teaching English for future trips to the West. When I complimented her on the magnificence of her Russian boots, he coughed in some embarrassment, "I bought them for her in Rome," he said. The three of us dined, and we all commiserated on the miseries of divorce, alimony, the alienation of one's children. He too is gone. Letters are unanswered. Questions to his successors such as, "What happened to old so-and-so?" are met with a shake of the head, a reply of, "I don't know," or, "I think he's in Kiev." Then the successors go too.

8

Whatever Happened to Philby & Co.?

Do you know the land where the lemons bloom?
There, there, I would like to go with you, beloved.

— GOETHE

Treason is a question of dates.

— TALLEYRAND

There exists in Moscow a little colony, rarely seen. The Western correspondents call it the colony of the "little gray men." They rather resemble the "halfway" suicide-pact couple in *Outward Bound*, neither living nor dead, rejected but not accepted into the other life. These are the Westerners who chose to throw in their lot with Stalin against their own people, and then stayed on. From the beginning they were aware that should armed conflict ever arise between the Soviet Union and the West they, despite their self-sacrifice on the altar of Communism, would be the first to be shot. Indeed, they take a rather grisly relish in saying so.

Their decision was made by a curious process of psychological self-immolation. Nearly all the defectors crossed the Iron Curtain (and détente or no détente, the curtain is still there, and it is still iron) during the harshest and most intractable days of

Stalin's Cold War. They feared the insecurities of freedom. They needed Big Brother to soothe away their fears.

At the time of their disappearance they caused an uproar in the newspapers of their home countries. Then they gradually disappeared from public consciousness and almost, it seems, from the act of living itself. Moscow, although a large city, has only a handful of cinemas, theaters and restaurants for its millions to go to. Yet the little gray men are under the orders of their unsympathetic bosses to remain invisible to Western eyes.

How they manage to avoid contact, particularly at the height of the tourist season, must be an agony in itself. One imagines them darting around corners when they see Westerners approaching, living the scruffy, overcrowded life of the Muscovites as far away as possible from the privileged compounds of the resident Westerners with their ample amenities. They must shun the Bolshoi Ballet and international restaurants like the Aragvi and the elegant Ararat.

As a compulsive expatriate, having lived in almost any country but my own throughout my adult life, I have always been fascinated by the subject of defection. While expatriation is merely adventure, defection is utter and irrevocable. Defection carries expatriation up to, and usually over, the borderline into treason. There is a little of the defector in us all, symbolized by the expression "The grass is always greener." We restrain it because we suspect that somewhere, over the rainbow, we will find something not better but worse, not fairy gold but dead leaves. It is the restraint that holds one to an unhappy marriage despite the temptations to try for a happy second.

In the first scene of Noel Coward's one-act play *Fumed Oak*, a henpecked little husband is bullied by his shrewish wife and equally shrewish daughter—ignored, half starved, yelled at. He accepts it all meekly. In the second scene he turns the tables and announces he is off to Latin America with a false passport, escaping from his monstrous suburban existence, with enough money to sustain him for the rest of his life in a paradise where the two hags could never find him. There the play ended, to applause and laughter from the audience for the good guy who won.

The implication was that the little man would spend his days sitting around tropical swimming pools in white ducks, sipping exotic drinks with lots of rum in them, or smoking Corona-Coronas while ladies all looking like Carmen Miranda danced the samba for him.

But if one takes the scene beyond the final curtain, the probabilities are quite the opposite. It is safer to presume that the little man would never master Spanish, never acquire a taste for garbanzos, never again get a good cup of tea, never fill in another football-pools coupon. There would be no dog to walk to the local pub for a chat with the lads and a game of shove ha'penny or darts. The only new friends he would make would be expatriates as miserable and homesick as he. In other words, disillusion and bitterness, and probably even a pining for nasty wife and daughter.

For the defectors to the East it is equally safe to presume that access to the special restricted department at GUM for hard-to-get merchandise; occasional cheap holidays at Sochi and Yalta; freedom to make a few telephone calls home to one's brother and sister (on the strict understanding that they tell *no one* about it, or the press will get on to it), and oceans and oceans of vodka do not in any way compensate for what they have abandoned. We know it. They know it. What makes it worse for them is that they know we know it. They cannot boast. They can only rationalize, and that only to themselves. Kim Philby's casual admission to Roy Blackman of the London *Daily Express* that he missed an occasional pint of bitter, or a sunny afternoon at Lords, is profounder than it sounds This is not small stuff. It is the essence of life and happiness.

A clue to the mystery of defection was first supplied me, not in Moscow but in East Berlin. I was having lunch in the East Berlin Press Club with John Peet. In 1950 Peet, while Reuters correspondent in West Berlin, suddenly defected to the East. A humorous, attractive, untidy man in his fifties, he runs an efficient and often witty Communist propaganda sheet called *German Democratic Report* from a cluttered office on Krauserstrasse, just on the wrong side of Checkpoint Charlie. Defection had not made Peet rich. His suit was nondescript, his Wartburg car battered.

My question to him was not so much, "Why did you defect?" but "Why *then?*" Why defect when the Berlin blockade and the Communist coup d'état in Czechoslovakia were recent news, revealing the bloody hand of Stalin?

His reply was, "It was not the Germany I was defecting to. It was the Germany I was defecting from." His answer could perhaps be argued as legitimate in the context of the time: the American rearming of West Germany, the fears of reemerging Nazism, the Gestapo-ish undertones of Adenauer's Secret Service under the sinister Richard Gehlen. But it is not legitimate now. West Germany under Brandt and subsequently Helmut Schmidt has perhaps the most sanely liberal régime in the Western world.

But at least John Peet *replied*, which is rare among defectors and almost unheard of among the Moscow colony of little gray men. But Archibald Johnstone replied too. As I mentioned, he had been Moscow editor of *British Ally*. Johnstone defected in 1949, followed less than a year later by his assistant editor, Robert Dalgleish.

Johnstone, in his thick Scottish accent, told me, "I quit because I dinna lake the boss classes. In Britain it's 'them' and 'us.'" He clearly did not include Joseph Stalin among the "thems."

But usually when one tracks down a defector, not an easy task in itself, the response is a shy, sly smile, a wink, and the implication, "Ah, my friend! If I told you the truth, God, how surprised you would be! It would turn your hair white. If I ever wrote it down on paper, no one in the world would believe it!"

A frequent reply to the question "Why?" is a jeering laugh

and a line like "Hah! Wouldn't the C.I.A. like to know!" A way-out and rather pathetic egotism which has to sustain the morale of people about whom the C.I.A. could not care less. They live in a dream in which they are central figures in the eye of the hurricane of world events, changing the course of history.

They honestly believe that should they suddenly materialize by enchantment in Regent Street or on Pennsylvania Avenue, there would be gasps and all heads would turn, with crowds parting for the police to push through, fangs dripping and hungry for arrest. It is an eerie twilight world, wavering uneasily on the edge of treason against their country, a world redolent of mystery, the presumed knowledge of dark secrets and similar ambiguous—and erroneous—givings out.

In fact there are usually two answers, sometimes more. A friend who knew John Peet better than I suggested that his decision to defect was not unconnected with domestic problems. Johnstone knew that the Soviet authorities were about to close down *British Ally* and was terrified of returning to the rat race of free enterprise and likely unemployment. He preferred Soviet security on a pittance, translating poetry for the Foreign Languages Publishing House, complaining that Mayakovsky was out of fashion. He liked translating Mayakovsky because Mayakovsky wrote staccato poetry with sometimes only two words to the line: Johnstone was paid by the line. He died secure and poor, an active member of Moscow's Robert Burns Society.

And even when the answer is simple, a second one has to be invented. The reason for the defection of Donald Maclean, Kim Philby, Donald Burgess and Professor Bruno Pontecorvo, the atom scientist, was simplicity itself. They were spies unmasked. But they have all rewritten their histories. Now it has something to do with American imperialism, Joe McCarthy, warmongering and peace on earth.

In his book *British Foreign Policy Since Suez*, published in London by Hodder & Stoughton, Donald Maclean explains his pell-mell flight from England as follows: "When, after sixteen years of my working life in the Diplomatic Service, I found myself faced with the necessity of finding a new profession, I decided after much casting around, that what I was best qualified to do was to contribute to this much wider problem by making a continuous study ... of the process of development of contemporary British foreign policy." Which is his way of explaining how he got out of the back door as the fuzz were coming in through the front to nick him as a spy.

Kim Philby's defection in 1962 was in many ways the most intriguing and bizarre of them all. Like Burgess and Maclean eleven years earlier, he defected because he had been fingered as a spy. More vividly than anyone else, he knew what he was letting himself in for, because Guy Burgess was his best friend and told him endlessly how miserable he was in Moscow. It was Philby, "the third man," who, while in the Foreign Office, told Burgess and Maclean urgently to split because their goose was cooked.

If Philby, in the comfort of Beirut in 1962, closed his eyes and thought of Burgess he saw a wretched man, wearing a borscht-stained Eton tie and threadbare Savile Row suit, permanently drunk, in a cramped, overheated two-room flat, each room the size of an average American apartment-house bathroom. His teeth had been kicked in by young Moscow bullies, whom he had probably importuned. He did not even own a car to help him escape into the countryside from the stifling claustrophobia of his life. The authorities decided he wasn't worth one, and took it away. His friends believe the shock and humiliation of that hastened his breakdown and death. Philby knew all this. Philby was forced to defect because he had been found out, but he actually went further than Burgess and Maclean. He renounced his British citizenship and became a Soviet citizen, which the other two never did.*

---

* Only in England ... When Burgess and Maclean defected in 1951, they disappeared completely for five years, living in Kuibishev, five hundred miles from Moscow. They reemerged in Moscow in 1956 for a brief press appearance. With this evidence of their continued existence, the British declared them

One can see why the big names dare not redefect—Sing Sing and Parkhurst offer prospects even less pleasing than the prospects of Moscow. The biggest American names are Alfred Stern and his wife Martha Dodd, who live not in Moscow but in Prague. They had been accused of being Soviet spies by the F.B.I. and fled. Martha Dodd, as the daughter of the United States ambassador to Hitler's Berlin, met Hitler and most of the Nazis. Stern, a millionaire, inherited a large fortune from his banking family in North Dakota. His first wife was the wealthy Marion Rosenwald, who later married Max Ascoli and helped him publish *The Reporter* magazine in Washington. They, and Philby and Maclean, have to stay put.

One would, however, think it comparatively easy for the many small fry to return home, but they too stay put. One reason was suggested in an excellent book, *A Room in Moscow* by Sally Belfrage, who spent a considerable time studying in the Soviet Union in the 1950s and was one of the few Westerners who managed to get to know certain defectors intimately.

According to Miss Belfrage, many of the expatriates were initially received with suspicion as possible spies. They had been ill used, imprisoned and sometimes tortured before achieving such limited acceptance as the Soviet authorities accord to people they instinctively despise. Miss Belfrage, bewildered, asked them why on earth they stayed. They explained to her that the Soviet Union was reluctant to grant exit visas to British, French or other nationals who would then go home and complain of brutality, spreading the story of their experiences in the mass newspapers. So exit visas were offered on the condition that they take out Soviet citizenship.

This is a wonderful demonstration of devious bureaucratic thinking, yet it has a certain wacky logic to it. Presumably the Soviet Union could then argue that what it does to its own

---

"nonresidents" of Britain. The result was that the dividends they received from stock they still owned became free of income tax. To the end of his life Burgess regularly telephoned his London stockbroker from Moscow.

citizens is its own business and has nothing to do with the Helsinki Agreement.

But the defectors are now seen to have caught it both ways. Suppose they accepted Soviet citizenship, and then the Soviet authorities turned around and refused them exit visas anyway. The visa office has changed its mind on all sorts of notorious occasions. So the defectors, fearing that they would be put even more at the mercy of the régime than they were before—and not believing a word the Russians tell them—preferred to keep their passports and stay miserable.

Some of the defectors are famous, even eminent, like Bruno Pontecorvo, Philby to a certain extent, and Dolores Ibaruri, "La Pasionaria" of the Spanish Civil War. La Pasionaria is more a refugee than à defector. In 1975, after thirty-six years in the Soviet Union, she turned up in Paris, hoping that a post-Franco régime would permit her to return to her native land.

Ivy Low Litvinov, widow of the Soviet Union's Foreign Secretary, Maxim Litvinov, has returned to spend the rest of her days in her native Britain after a lifetime in the Soviet Union. Mme. Litvinov knows more secrets about the history of the Soviet Union since its inception than anybody else in the world. One hopes that the story will be written.

Dennis Vinscottski, once Dennis Winscott, bears a claim to fame as one of the ringleaders of the Royal Navy mutiny at Invergordon in 1932. He opted to emigrate to the Soviet Union and has lived there ever since. He served in the Red Army during the war and spent a term in one of Stalin's jails as a suspected spy.

But most are obscure people, working anonymously in the Foreign Languages Publishing House. Some of the brighter ones are employed by Novosti. A few with suitably B.B.C.-type voices are used by Moscow Radio in its English-language broadcasts to extol Soviet factory production.

The British colony pines for Britain but, like Archie Johnstone, is terrified at the initiative that would be required to return to and survive in a free society. The free education and free medical care are constantly stressed when its members talk to Westerners. But teatime ritual is observed as faithfully as it ever was in the outer stations of the British Empire.

The late René MacColl of the London *Daily Express* recalled how one defector recognized him, rushed up, was struck almost dumb by the torrent of questions he longed to ask, and all he could stammer out was, "And tell me ... h-h-how ... how are things in Golders Green?"—a question which MacColl found truly sad.

I was given limited access to the set because one of its members was longing for up-to-date gossip on cricket. He trembled for it, the way Ben Gunn pined for cheese on Treasure Island. He asked me to call him "just Jimmie" and said several times, "I am very grateful to the Soviet Union for allowing me to stay here." He was not interested in the scores and standings; he heard all those on the B.B.C. World Service, to which every defector listens avidly. He wanted gossip and spicy tidbits about the players, and the more scabrous the better. Happily I was able to supply him with just enough to give the addict a temporary high, and one of the spinoffs was a brief session with Donald Maclean.

The backbiting and community hatred that goes on among this tiny bunch of frustrated and imprisoned expatriates can be well imagined. One of the poetic justices of history is that Burgess and Maclean, two names as inextricably linked as Burke and Hare or Laurel and Hardy, who escaped Britain, as it were, hand in hand, grew in Moscow to detest each other passionately. Although Maclean was ordered by the commissars to attend Burgess's funeral, in life he avoided Burgess as much as he could. When asked about Burgess, Maclean would reply, "I never see him." When asked about Maclean, Burgess replied, "That bastard."

I do believe that Nikita Khrushchev's denunciation of Stalin in 1956 (which has still never been reported officially in the

Soviet Union) was less of a sensation in the colony of defectors than Melinda Maclean's decision to leave her husband and move in with Kim Philby. Maclean had always been resented and envied. He held a responsible position in the Soviet Foreign Office (and one carefully excluded from direct Western contact). It is believed that when Andrey Gromyko, the Foreign Secretary, had something sophisticated he wanted to say in English, it was to Maclean's office that he looked for *le mot juste.*

In comparison, Guy Burgess, Archie Johnstone and Robert Dalgleish were shunted off to the menial task of translation. Translation, in itself, does not sound too uninteresting, but when one sees the works the authorities want translated into English, the expression "bored to death" takes on literal significance. How would you like to translate into English the speeches at the annual congress of the Uzbekistan Communist Party?

Humiliation seems to be an essential part of the Moscow defectors' existence, both in the office and in private life, and it is almost impossible to avoid concluding that the Soviet Foreign Office authorities rather enjoy watching the hapless foreigners squirm. Donald Maclean humiliated Guy Burgess by his superior position in the Soviet hierarchy. He also humiliated Ralph Parker by coming to Moscow in the first place. Parker was, from the start, one of the odder birds in the Moscow nest. He made the curious switch from the Moscow bureau of the London *Times* to the Moscow bureau of *The New York Times* to the Moscow bureau of the Communist *Daily Worker* (today the *Morning Star*). At the end of his life he was scattering his prose around the London *New Statesman* and the *Times of India.*

He married a Russian girl, acquired an inordinate taste for vodka and threw in his lot with the Communists. Many correspondents believe it was Ralph Parker who dreamed up the propaganda idea of accusing the United States of using germ warfare in North Korea. James Cameron, the British foreign correspondent and author, saw Parker at the Bandung Conference in Djakarta, Indonesia, and recalled him as "seemingly ill, and in a sort of inner despair."

Parker never tried to hide his resentment of Maclean. Indeed, resentment is one sentiment no one seems to hide in Moscow, whether native or immigrant. But then, Maclean was the next to feel humiliation when his wife, Melinda, left him for Kim Philby.

Shortly afterward it was Philby's turn. When George Blake, the British spy, escaped dramatically from prison in England where he was serving a 40-year term for treason, he turned up in Moscow. Philby, the star defector, took him rather patronizingly under his wing. He introduced Blake to his earlier wife, Eleanor, once married to Sam Pope Brewer of *The New York Times*, and he introduced him to Melinda.

Then Blake humiliated Kim Philby. Blake was awarded the prestigious Order of Lenin, an award which had been denied to Philby, who had only received the lesser Order of the Red Banner. Blake, it must be remembered, had been a minor official in the British Foreign Office, while Philby had been the head of the American desk itself. The anger and social embarrassment of Philby, who considered himself, and was indeed considered by the rest, to be the number one glamour-boy defector, could be imagined.

But no one is exempt from Moscow's psychological knout. Blake had always been the one defector totally inaccessible to Western newsmen. The others *could* be approached if one worked at it hard enough. Blake's remoteness was considered for a long time to be indication of his importance in Russian eyes. But then he was given a job which was leaked to the West—translation for the Foreign Languages Publishing House! The rubbish heap had acquired a new empty shell.

The Western authorities are also not beyond joining in the pastime of making Red faces redder. Robert Dalgleish, unlike his former boss, Archie Johnstone, retained his British passport. When he decided to marry a Russian girl who had worked as a switchboard operator at the British Embassy he had the chutzpah to exert his right as a British subject to get married at the embassy. Traditionally the ambassador himself performs such pleasant little ceremonies. On this occasion Ambassador Sir William Hayter decided he had other duties and delegated the task to a lesser official. There was no reception afterward.

Maclean was repeatedly described to me by Jimmie, my cricketing friend, as "the man who played second fiddle to the Third Man." Maclean lives in a sixth-floor apartment on the Shevchenko Boulevard on the Moskva River, and the living room has a fine view of the Foreign Office wedding-cake skyscraper. He is still exceptionally handsome, though graying, but he has run somewhat thick, and his posture is stooped, as is often the case with very tall men. I visited him with Roy Blackman of the *Daily Express.*

Maclean was wearing an old flannel dressing gown and tattered Soviet pajamas, and he rebuked us mildly when we knocked for interrupting the B.B.C. news. He was so anxious not to admit us into his apartment that he succeeded in locking all three of us out, and we had to wait in an unheated corridor in the middle of a Moscow January until his babushka returned from walking his dog, Scamp.

This desperate, physical barring of the front door to Westerners is common to defectors all over Eastern Europe. In Prague I couldn't get in the home of Alfred Stearns and his wife, the former Martha Dodd. In East Berlin, Colin Lawson of the *Daily Express* was refused entrance to Alan Winnington's flat. (Winnington had covered the Korean War from the North Korean side for the London *Daily Worker.*) This shyness stems from a determination not to reveal the tatty conditions in which they live, and from the certain knowledge that every word spoken inside is bugged and that the whole sordid scene will be reported in the American and British press by whichsoever journalist gets his foot in the door.

Despite the annoyance of our unwelcome presence and with

his nose turning blue, Maclean was courteous and reprimanded us only mildly, "You might have telephoned first." (Blackman, aside to me, "And he would have said he was too busy.")

Maclean was also wholly uncommunicative. He said he was working at the Academy of Science, "not exactly digging with a spade," he added. He touched his forehead. "Still using the old gray matter."

Blackman smoothly asked a loaded question. "Doing any travels abroad these days?"

Maclean paused only momentarily. What Blackman meant, and what Maclean knew perfectly well he meant, was that if he put his nose in the West, Interpol would grab him at the airport and dispatch him to London, where he would be tried at the Old Bailey for treason, a prospect which always terrifies the bigger defectors. Maclean countered with what the chess correspondent of *The New York Times* might have called the Damascus Gambit. He said, "There are plenty of places in the Soviet Union I haven't seen yet. Goodbye, gentlemen, I see my dog and my babushka have returned."

"Poor bugger," said Blackman as we walked back to his apartment, both our faces purple with cold. "When Moscow drives *us* crazy, when we feel we can't breathe anymore, we call our Foreign Desk, get the nod and fly out for a spot of London night life, or the Riviera. For these people there is no escape."

I tried, without success, to see Philby. I set eyes on him only once, but under circumstances which perhaps add a microscopic footnote to history. In 1962, several months before Philby defected, I was having drinks with various Western correspondents in the bar of the Intercontinental Hotel in Beirut. Philby came in with another group and sat at a table. One of the men in my group, an American, called, "Hi, Kim! How's the espionage biz?" Philby laughed heartily.

Back briefly to Ralph Parker, and my own experience with him. I was in Moscow to do an article about Soviet film stars for the *Saturday Evening Post*. It was surely as innocuous a story as one could be asked to do; I had no intention of asking how long they had spent in Stalin's concentration camps or about parents disappearing in the purges. But in those days, before the Novosti Press Agency existed to set up facilities—at a price—it needed contacts through all sorts of snaillike bureaucratic channels, each one passing the buck until the final "*nyet.*" (In actuality, *nyet* is very rarely used, contrary to Western belief. The answer is always, "The person you want is not here. I don't know when he will come back.")

To seek a short cut I telephoned Wilfrid Burchett, Moscow correspondent for the French Communist daily *L'Humanité.* I had once worked with him on the *Daily Express.* Burchett was out of town, so I made contact with Ralph Parker.

We met in the restaurant of the Hotel Metropole. He was a big, unsmiling, suspicious man, wearing a stained, old-fashioned double-breasted English suit and a shirt from GUM. The eggplant color of his nose indicated tastes which I satisfied with "a hundred grams of vodka" (that's how they order drinks in Moscow). Parker had not much longer to live. He had long since ceased to be a big shot in the hierarchy of defectors, and, serving the Soviet Union no useful purpose, he had been tossed on to the scavenger belt of translation. I offered him a hundred dollars if he could get me into the Mosfilm Studios. It was not an ungenerous offer for a task which required only a couple of telephone calls to the right people.

Parker, however, was visibly uneasy, looking over his shoulder, although at 4 P.M. the restaurant was almost empty. He accepted a second hundred grams of vodka and drew heavily on his Russian cigarette. He said, "There is only one man in Moscow who can help you: Victor Louis." Louis, as mentioned earlier, is the rather mysterious Soviet citizen who acts as an unofficial link between the Western press and the Soviet authorities. Officially he is Moscow correspondent for the London *Evening News.* Parker gave me the telephone number without having to consult his own book and, after a third hundred grams of vodka, lumbered off.

I went straight to my room in the same hotel to dial (telephones in all Moscow Intourist hotels have direct dialing system). But evidently Parker had got to the telephone first and said something to the effect that, "There's an Englishman with an Italian name working for the Americans, ready to give you a hundred dollars to get into Mosfilm Studios."

I made a date with Louis to meet him at his apartment. He opened the door and held out his hand, which I shook. This was not what he had in mind. "Where," he asked, "is the hundred dollars?" As payment in advance did not seem to me to be particularly reasonable, the deal did not go through. Victor Louis, being Russian, then acted with characteristic hospitality and invited me to dinner. I eventually got my story anyway, and Louis subsequently described me to other Western correspondents as "that limey wop." The story is worth telling if only because it demonstrates the *totality* of suspicion among the little gray men.

To veteran Moscow defectors, the most baffling of all was Lee Harvey Oswald, the assassin of President Kennedy, a loner who made no sense even in the topsy-turvy logic of defection. As my cricket fan put it to me, "This fellow was a weirdo. The Soviet Union can recognize a weirdo as quickly as anyone else. Not only do they allow him in, which is ridiculous, they allow him to marry, which is unheard of. Not only do they allow him to marry, they allow him to marry a girl with major education, in which the Soviet Union has invested capital. The Soviet Union is insanely possessive of its educated classes, which is why it makes emigration as difficult as possible. And then the authorities allow them both *out*, which is mind-boggling. Meanwhile, many sober, upright, true-blue Marxist would-be defectors can't even get in."

Everyone has his personal theory about the Kennedy assassination. My own is that the Russians, recognizing possibilities in the psychopath, programmed Oswald to kill, like the assassin in Richard Condon's *Manchurian Candidate*. But one of the wires crossed. The puppet shuttled around out of control and blew the wrong man's brains out.

Two other Americans who upset the general pattern of defection were the code clerks Bernon F. Mitchell and William Martin, who defected in 1960, when they were thirty-one and twenty-nine respectively. They had worked three years for the supersecret National Security Agency in Washington, and their defection forced a deeply mortified Pentagon to change all its codes.

The two men gave a press conference at the House of Journalists in Moscow and said everything that the Pentagon hoped would be left unsaid by Americans. They defected, they said, when they discovered that American agents spied on friendly as well as unfriendly countries; that the C.I.A. provided money and military hardware to overthrow unfriendly governments (we all know this to be true now), and that United States policy was a build-up for a preventive war which would leave them "emperors over the graveyard of civilization." Then, having delivered Russia's blow into the American solar plexus, the pair disappeared into the obscurity which the Soviet Union reserves for turncoats with no further purpose. They are still around there, somewhere, poor wretches. One is said to have married.

The family tree of the major defectors, as we have now seen, is heavily intertwined. At the time of writing it stands as follows:

KIM PHILBY

Philby's wife, Eleanor, joined him in Moscow. She quickly realized that he was up to no good with Melinda Maclean, returned to the United States, and later died.

Two observations may be made about Philby's marriage to Melinda. One is that Philby had betrayed everybody and everything he could find: his country, his colleagues, his class, his education, his allies. Finding himself in Moscow with time on his hands, there was only one person left he could betray, his friend, so he did what came naturally.

The second observation (without being ungallant to a very attractive woman) is that Melinda Maclean is a lady *d'un certain age*, and Philby's selection scarcely flattered the available Russian talent. Eventually, of course, he did ditch Melinda to marry a young Russian woman, and so remained in character. According to those who have seen him, he is permanently sozzled.*

MELINDA MACLEAN

Lives in Moscow. Works on translations, receives *The New York Times* daily and, in 1973, suffered a mild heart attack.

DONALD MACLEAN

The Macleans' daughter, Mimsie, married a Russian boy, divorced him and lives in Moscow. Their son returned to England to complete his education. It would be unfair to invade privacy further.

GUY BURGESS

Burgess died in 1965 at the age of fifty-two. His ashes were flown to West Meon, Hampshire, where they now rest.

GEORGE BLAKE

Blake became a spy for the Communists when he was, of all things, a British civilian prisoner of war of the North Koreans. He has completely disappeared. Philby and Maclean are seen around town very occasionally, Blake never. Incidentally, whenever Philby is accosted by Westerners he replies in Russian, "I don't speak English," and hurries on.

* True story: Philby can be very funny. When the Beatles received their O.B.E. from the Queen, Philby professed himself outraged. He said, "The award has been debased! I am going to return my own O.B.E. immediately."

So we see the terrible anticlimax. What began as sincere ideology and proceeded to a desperate, romantic, dangerous decision, ended up as a miserable pay check for a lousy job. Again, why?

George Feifer, the most perceptive of all observers of contemporary Russia, said in his book *Message from Moscow*, "Russia has a unique ability to stimulate foreign interest, even love. Perhaps because of the universality of its great literature and art, perhaps because of its size, strength and a kind of purity, Russia represents the human condition and struggle of the human spirit more vividly than our own countries. We are fascinated by what is here; we want to be part of the struggle. We *personally* and often *involuntarily* identify with this people's difficulties and fate." The italics are mine.

I referred earlier to Donald Maclean's statement to Roy Blackman: "There are still plenty of places I haven't seen in the Soviet Union." The remark recalls a theme that has persisted throughout this book—the need of Westerners to get away, if only for a while; to escape the symbolic odor of Soviet gasoline, and to feel free air between finger and thumb. They can board the first plane west and return after they have drawn breath. The defectors are in prison for life, free to go from place to place "in the Soviet Union," with the smell following them everywhere.

9

Muscovites and the Pill

The wife of a Swedish businessman in this fair city told me the following almost incredible story. As she left the Hotel Rossiya one fall day she was accosted by a young woman of nondescript appearance, aged about thirty. The Swedish lady had been stopped many times before and presumed the woman wanted to buy her clothes or exchange rubles for her Swedish crowns at a discount rate. The Russian, however, rang an unexpected change on the familiar Moscow routine. What she said was, "I would like to buy from you all the birth control pills you can spare."

The Swede considered the pros and cons, and not least the risk to the woman herself of the proposition. Finally she asked, quite worried, "You are aware, are you not, that if you start taking the pill, you must take it every day?"

"I am."

"But why?"

"Because I need them."

"What I mean is . . . abortion is perfectly legal in the Soviet Union. If you find yourself pregnant, they perform the operation without question."

"Not in my case. If I go back to them *again*, I will have to leave Moscow. I don't want to spend the rest of my life in Tomsk."

"But even if I can help you, how then do you maintain your supply when it runs out?"

"The way I am doing now."

I don't know whether the Swedish lady supplied them or not. The Russians who accost Westerners in Moscow by definition live dangerously. Even so, this approach seemed to be taking rather more chances than most would dare. It also seemed to be an awfully precarious way to enjoy sex in any kind of security, rushing out every week or month to top up one's supply by panhandling Western women.

But in Russia nothing is ever the same as elsewhere. Soviet sex, like everything else, is a matter of concern in the government, and one's life in bed is something which demands government interference. Though it is never said so publicly, Russians always seem to know.

In 1969, after years of silence and cautious experiment, the Soviet state and its senior medical authorities began to come to terms with the Pill. Medical magazines predicted that 3 million women a year would shortly be receiving it. But the future role of the Pill, one can safely predict, will be a totally different one in Russia from what it has been in the West.

To begin with, there is no population explosion in the Soviet Union as yet, so the demand is comparatively small. Twenty million Russians were killed by the Germans in the Second World War, mostly young men. This has led to an excess of fatherless, single-child families, the father having been killed before he could have more children. Nureyev and Makarova, the two Leningrad ballet stars who defected to the West, are both war children in this category.

These solitary children usually want to have several children of their own to compensate for the loneliness and tragedy of their own childhood. Young couples make few demands on the clinics for instruction in birth control. Secondly, abortions are practiced freely in Russia and they cast no moral stigma on either the doctor or the woman concerned.

To learn the scientific standpoint, I called at the Scientific Institute of Midwifery and Gynecology in Moscow and talked to

Dr. Galina Truyestseva, head of the endocrinological laboratory there. I discovered to my surprise that there is no hard party line but actually several areas of dispute among doctors there. Dr. Galina (she attends many international conferences in western Europe, and friends and colleagues there find the name Truyestseva too much of a tongue-twister) is a petite, lively woman of middle age who speaks fluent English. She told me there would have to be basic changes in the pattern of Russian society before the Pill moves into everyday use. Sitting next to her, however, was a colleague, Dr. Olga Nikonchika, who more or less declared her political attitudes by her lipstick, which was the color of the Red Flag. Dr. Nikonchika believed in larger and larger families, and the superiority of Soviet morality. (*mon oeil:* author)

Dr. Galina said that while the Pill was an unimportant social and moral factor in the Soviet Union, she could see a situation some years hence when students and young people generally learned what a liberating influence it could have in their lives. Then, she said, while Dr. Olga shook her head, the Russian authorities would be faced with problems similar to those in capitalist countries.

"I prefer the Pill to abortion," said Dr. Galina, "but at the moment we prescribe it only to certain women who, for health or psychological reasons, should not get pregnant. No girl can simply present herself at this laboratory and demand the Pill just for her own convenience."

Yet sexual relations outside marriage are widespread in the Soviet Union, especially in student and intellectual circles. Officially any girl of eighteen and over can do as she pleases. And although what Dr. Galina calls rather coyly "prewedding practices" are not encouraged, there is certainly no law against them. The scenes in Gorky Park and Sokolniki Park in a hot Moscow summer make even London's Hyde Park, which so shocked Billy Graham, seem like Forest Lawn. Prostitutes prowl the railway stations. The Communist Revolution and then the

Second World War had a curious effect on Soviet women. The determination of Stalin to sublimate sex into tractor worship had the result of retarding their sexual sophistication. They are emancipated but not up to date. They are like women in a Tolstoy novel or a Chekhov play: romantic, artistic, sensitive and quick to tears.

Even an unmarried woman may be given a prescription for the Pill if the doctors decide that it would be dangerous for her to get pregnant. And an unmarried woman who does get pregnant will be given an abortion without question. But there are many bridges to cross before she can afford the luxury of even thinking about the Pill. First of all, there is such limited opportunity for lovemaking, which is discussed in another chapter. Apartments are overcrowded and claustrophobic. Hotels, motels, drive-ins and motor cars are nonexistent for the purpose.

Consequently, arrangements have to be prepared in advance—and elaborately. A couple may wait until their parents are away or at work. Once indoors they are reasonably safe—unless Grandmother decides to look in and clean the place up, as Russian grandmothers are wont to do. But they must beware of being seen coming or going because, on its more bourgeois levels, Soviet society is puritanical to the point of being positively snoopy, and the dreadful crime would be reported at once.

As indicated elsewhere, the suffocating atmosphere in Russian apartments, induced by the cramped space and the airlessness of the central heating, really has to be experienced to be believed. Outside, doors bang deafeningly (believe it or not, there are no swinging doors in the Soviet Union.) , winter boots crash on stairs, and one imagines one can hear the breathing in the next apartment of the neighbor whose ear is glued to the wall.

Another inhibition is fear, less of Big Brother than of Big Mother. More than 80 percent of doctors in Russia are women.

This is not, as many Westerners believe, because of losses in the war. Since the 1917 Revolution the Russians have always adhered to the view that a woman understands pain better than a man and is gentler with the sick—a point of view I disagree with violently. Women doctors are also inclined to take a more sternly moral attitude to a young woman's sex escapades.

A further inhibition is the dread of exile. A single woman who gets pregnant and receives an abortion commits no crime, but there is a blot on her escutcheon that is not forgotten. She must be especially cautious from then on. If she gets a reputation for being immoral, all sorts of disagreeable things can happen to her. She can lose her job, her enrollment in the university and such living space as she has.

There is no unemployment in the Soviet Union, so the state owes her a duty to find her a job elsewhere. But the twist in the story lies in the word "elsewhere." Conditions are grim, indeed, in Novosibirsk or Irkutsk. Young Russians pine for Moscow as ardently as Chekhov's Olga, Masha and Irina. Moscow is the swinging city where the action is, and outside Moscow, the magic talisman of the language is *propuska*, the document permitting one to take up residence in Moscow. As one Latvian student at Moscow University told me, "Beyond Moscow's city limits, in any direction, is Siberia."

All these inhibitions add up to the fact that Russians are compelled to be as secretive about love as about so many other things, speaking frankly only occasionally in talks with friendly Westerners, and then usually after several vodkas. The lack of opportunity leads not so much to frustration as to a kind of acceptance.

Whereas in the West people talk about sex, read about sex, see sex endlessly in the movies, on the stage and television, the Russians just don't. The best analogy is that they avoid talking about sex the way, in the West, one avoids talking about lavatory matters. It is just not *kulturny*. Young Russians *en masse* cannot understand Western preoccupation with the subject. The time devoted elsewhere to kissing and lovemaking is channeled in Russia into talk, so that even Moscow working-class girls tend to be witty and flip, with quick, original answers to everything.

These are factors, of course, which have nothing to do with the beliefs of Drs. Galina Truyestseva and Olga Nikonchika. How far Russia must go to be aware of the Pill and its repercussions was illustrated indirectly to me during my long talk with the two women doctors. I had been allotted, as aide, translator and K.G.B. watchdog, a pretty woman in her twenties whom I will call Asya. Asya speaks English perfectly, and she is an experienced journalist with Novosti. She has enough access to the Western press to be familiar with current trends, especially in fashion.

Neither Asya nor I realized that Dr. Galina spoke such idiomatic English, so what might have been a stiff and slow interview turned into an agreeable and sometimes hilarious chat over coffee, biscuits and plum brandy in a most pleasant flower-decked consulting room. Even Dr. Olga's party-line interjections occasionally caused us all merriment.

But as the conversation progressed I regarded Asya with increasing curiosity and interest. I had briefed her in advance about what I wanted to know, but she had misunderstood and thought we were to talk about pills in general. It was clear that the word Pill with a capital letter meant absolutely nothing to her, and I had had, with a certain amount of embarrassment, to explain it to her briefly. But as she listened to the conversation she showed increasing astonishment. Occasionally I thought I detected a blush on her pink, slightly frostbitten cheeks.

Now here was a girl who by almost any standards in the world was sophisticated, worldly, highly educated and extremely well informed. She was doing well in the very tough business of journalism—the fact that she was moonlighting with the K.G.B. and reporting to them about my activities was neither here nor there; that was her job. She met people in all walks of life, Russian and Western. She had even lived for several years in China, "deeply regretted" what had happened between the two countries and saw no hope of any improvement in the relations.

But there was a sizable gap in her knowledge. It was obvious, and she admitted it to me afterward in the street, that while she knew about birth control, much of what she heard at the interview was news to her and not a little shocking. And it was only later that I learned she was engaged to be married.

If Asya only knew in the vaguest terms about the Pill, how much further behind are the rest of Russian womanhood, and how long will they take to catch up in Vladivostok?

"Tell me, Mr. Bocca," Dr. Olga boomed heartily, "have you visited beautiful Sochi and Yalta and our other Crimean resorts?"

"No, Dr. Olga," I replied. "It seems that every time I get to Moscow I always find so much to do and so many people to see that I never seem able to get beyond the ring roads."

"You must," said Dr. Olga. "They are the most beautiful resorts in the world, and the climate is so healthy it turns the old into the young."

I said, "Frankly, Dr. Olga, I do not feel a great temptation to visit Yalta or Sochi, except for educational purposes, because my home is on the French Riviera, so it would be rather like taking coals to Newcastle. I prefer the contrasts of Moscow and Leningrad, and to study the influence of nineteenth-century architecture which the Russian grand dukes imposed on the city of Nice."

"Riviera, pooh!" said Dr. Olga. "Our Crimean resorts are much superior."

As I had never been to the Crimea, and I was prepared to wager that Dr. Olga had never visited the Côte d'Azur, I did not think we were progressing, and I even sensed a certain hostility, so I said in a mollifying tone to end the subject, "But on the Riviera, we also have the benefit of the French cuisine, especially Provençale cuisine."

I then found I had not ended something—I had started something.

"Cuisine!" Dr. Olga exclaimed. "Don't talk about something you know nothing about, young man. The Russian cuisine is far better."

There are some remarks so incredible that they crack the carapace of the politest of intercourse. "You must be joking," I said, after my fit of coughing had subsided and the plum brandy had rediverted itself into the right canal. Even Dr. Olga seemed to feel she had gone rather far, and she added defensively, "Not in the restaurants, perhaps, but certainly in private houses."

I thought of the cabbage smells of Moscow apartment houses, of the unappetizing groceries which Muscovites refrigerate between their double windows in the winter. I remembered the mouth-watering aromas one savors every midday as one walks along the main street of the French village in which I live, and I said firmly, "Let us get back on the subject. What will happen when the Soviet Union wakes up to the fact of the Pill?"

Dr. Olga believed that the Soviet Union was bigger than the Pill, and that the innate morality of Soviet young people, guided by the teachings of Lenin and the wisdom of the party, would prevail. Dr. Galina said she thought it needed an indoctrination process that might take five to ten years. Asya offered no opinion.

"At the moment," said Dr. Galina, "the demand can be satisfied in the laboratories. The critical moment will come if and when we have to turn the laboratories into factories. It is perhaps not a mixed blessing that our Pill is not very satisfactory, and we import a lot from Hungary. How many can such a small country as Hungary produce?"

"Fascinating," said Asya outside in the freezing cold. "I really enjoyed meeting the two doctors. Quite an eye-opener. And by the way, my father thanks you very much for those lovely Wilkinson razor blades which you gave me. Apart from almost gashing himself to death the first time he used them, he says he has never had such marvelous shaves. My father also asked me to give you this."

And she produced a charming, hand-carved peasant pipe, which I treasure. As I have said before, it is almost impossible to give a Russian any kind of present without being given something in return.

"Please thank your father very much," I said. "He is most kind."

I had given Asya the blades a day or so earlier. She said then how pleased her father would be. Always her father, her father, her father. I think that on this particular visit to Moscow I saw Asya almost every day. We lunched and went to the theater, and I analyzed her in terms of a gigantic father complex. And then, not more than three weeks later, back in my home in France, I received a card from her, announcing her wedding.

She had never once mentioned that she was engaged, or even acknowledged, the existence of a boy friend. This would be understandable if she were following orders from Novosti or the K.G.B. But then, why write me at all? This is just one more example of how Russian behavior is so incomprehensible to Westerners. Once again, as so often in this book, I am obliged to report without being able to explain.

10

The Girls of Moscow

Ah, Asya! Will one ever solve the mystery of Muscovite womanhood? By the time I received her wedding announcement, I had long since become immune to surprise on the subject. A writer, before World War II, said that there are thousands of beautiful Russian women, but not one between Paris and Shanghai. There is a considerable basis for the claim that there is little feminine allure in the Soviet Union, but the statement implies that all the beauties left at the Revolution. What is truer is that they seem to find themselves only when they leave the Soviet Union.

Take Natalia Makarova. Before she quit the Kirov Ballet she presumably was a dowdy gray mouse like the rest of the company, shepherded into chartered buses by the traveling commissars, shunning contact with Westerners, avoiding the press, coming to life only on stage. The moment Makarova defected she burst out of not one cocoon but two—the Soviet Union's and her own. Almost overnight she became the most temperamental prima donna since Maria Callas, cordially detested by choreographer, partner and corps de ballet alike. And she also revealed an inner glamour as hot as fire.

One simply has to take Russian womanhood as one finds it, and be prepared for surprises.

Irina was twenty-two years old when I met her so, as I write, she must be thirty. Her love, like that of so many Russians, was poetry. She showed me a copy of a book she had just queued up to buy. It was a collection of the love poems of Anna Akhmatova, and it had been published only the week before I had arrived in Moscow. Until then it had been unattainable since the Russian Revolution.

The story of Akhmatova is a fascinating one. She died in 1968. Before the First World War she lived in Paris and was painted by Modigliani. Her poems, dealing with physical love, had a considerable success. She was in Leningrad, or Petrograd, at the time of the Revolution, and although she escaped the firing squads she never compromised with the régime.

Her flowing cloak and eccentric appearance were a familiar sight on the Leningrad scene, even though her books, unfortunately, were not. For forty years she was banned because the régime found her work "erotic," "decadent" and "religio-mystical." She was saved from starvation by loyal Leningrad publishers, who gave her work as a translator, as they did for Boris Pasternak.

She was in Leningrad during the siege in World War II with her female companion, and they burned all their furniture to keep from freezing to death. After the war Zhdanov denounced Akhmatova as "not quite a nun, not quite a wanton, but both a wanton and a nun," and said that her writing was "the poetry of an agitated lady, tossing about in her dreams between the boudoir and the chapel, and not knowing which she will select." She remained, however, an intimate of the intellectuals such as Pasternak, Zoschenko and Tvardovsky, editor of *Novy Mir*.

It is impossible for us in the West to understand the pressures on Moscow intellectuals. One can understand why distinguished scientists can be threatened and bulldozed into condemning Andrey Sakharov after he was awarded the Nobel Peace Prize in 1974. One can appreciate the despair of Maya Plissetskaya, forced to sign a petition that was deeply repugnant to her.

But there are other issues, less black and white. Nikolay Sholokov, Nobel prize winner and author of (or was he?

Solzhenytsin declares otherwise) *And Quiet Flows the Don* was a particular favorite of Nikita Khrushchev. During Khrushchev's years of power, Sholokov accompanied him on his junkets to the West. After Khrushchev's downfall Sholokov was silent, and he did not attend the funeral of his former mentor. Political pressure? Or playing safe?

When Larissa Daniel, fragile wife of the dissident author, was sentenced to carrying logs in Siberia, a task far beyond her strength, the prison authorities let it be known that if publishers were to send her books for translation, she would be freed for the task. Mme. Daniel speaks fluent English and German. Moscow publishers are as sensitive as men of letters anywhere in the world. Yet not a single manuscript was sent to her.

Back to Irina. When we met at the Budapest Restaurant, Akhmatova's poems had just been "rehabilited," not in a tiny edition which is the Communist way of getting unwelcome writers out of their hair, but in a substantial edition of fifty thousand copies. Irina had stormed the lines of students at the bookstores and had acquired a copy. What impressed me as much as the publication of Akhmatova's works at all was Irina's familiarity with them. She could quote them at length, even though she had just bought the book that afternoon.

"If Anna Akhmatova's work has not been published in the Soviet Union for forty years," I asked Irina, "and presumably were proscribed in the libraries, how on earth do you know her poetry so well?"

Of one thing I was already sure, from repeated experience. Whatever answer I was about to receive would only make my confusion more complete. I was right.

"Oh!" Irina said, with a shrugging of the shoulders, almost as though the question were too silly to merit an answer. "We learn."

The Russian girl has an absolute genius for intellectual and diplomatic evasion. Asya, for example, was a ballet fanatic, and we discussed the various Bolshoi dancers throughout an entire luncheon at the Ararat. At the end I tossed in the firecracker I had held back. "What do you think of Nureyev?"

If I had hoped to catch her, which I had, I failed. Asya flashed me a brilliant smile. "He is Kirov," she said, "Leningrad. We are talking about the Bolshoi. Moscow."

Twilight comes to darken the ambers, greens, the Schönbrun yellows of Moscow's buildings, and snow falls out of a charcoal sky on the cheeks of the Muscovite hordes hurrying home along Gorky Street and Sverdlovsk Square toward the Metros. This is the time when one becomes most acutely aware of the phenomenon which never fails to astonish, and appall, Western visitors. Old grandmothers, muffled in scarves and waddling about in great gray felt boots, emerge with witches' brooms to sweep the snow from the sidewalks. The task would be hard enough for lumberjacks, and in the United States these old ladies would be sitting in rockers, occasionally indulging in such intense physical activity as making apple pie. These old street sweepers—together with the Amazons who handle pneumatic drills as though they were toothpicks, with the ladies who service the aircraft of Aeroflot, with the female athletes who tend to swing Olympic Games for the Soviet Union, have formed the image of the Russian woman in the mind of the West: an image of toughness, shapelessness and sexlessness.

The image could not be more false. Russian women themselves are ashamed of their women streetcleaners and blame their existence on the war—women exceed men in the Soviet Union by tens of millions. The West has had plenty of opportunity to see that other kinds of Russian women exist. We have seen the Bolshoi and the Stanislavsky actresses. We have stars like Tatyana Samoilova and the Ukrainian sex kitten, Shanna Prokorenko, in *Ballad of a Soldier*.

Western ballet is graced by Natalia Makarova and Galina Samtsova of the London Festival Ballet. (Samtsova, incidentally, is the only Soviet dancer in the West who returns regularly to the Soviet Union for guest appearances. This is because she married a Canadian when she was with the Kiev Ballet and left the country with official permission.) The film *Andrey Rublev*, produced at great cost in 1969 and then, not surprisingly, banned in the Soviet Union, illustrates that Russian actresses are just as ready to take off all their clothes as Western and even Czech actresses.

These, of course, are exceptions. The actresses and dancers are privileged personalities and have access to better beauty aids and higher-quality clothes. But there are thousands of pretty girls in Moscow and many beautiful women, as I have indicated earlier. In Moscow women have to fight a constant battle to stay attractive in the face of the most depressing odds. The fashion magazines are a joke. Moscow lipstick has the texture of butterscotch. Face powder is like flour. Dresses that would be scorned by any self-respecting department store cost more than a hundred dollars, so workers usually buy material and have their dresses made up by seamstresses. This, in too many instances, is a case of the blind leading the blind. Shoes of absurd design cost sixty dollars. Until quite recently hairdressers were a definite menace, and many women suffered bad burns.

Most of the feminine acquaintances I made in Moscow, at one period, I met through an artist friend called Boris—at least I shall call him Boris. On more recent visits I failed to find any trace of him, but that again is a common experience in this most mysterious and anonymous of all cities. He was thirty-five years old, a bachelor, good-looking, very pale, with unkempt, wavy black hair, usually in need of a shampoo.

He loved to talk seriously about modern art, and he and I walked for hours through the Pushkin Museum. The Pushkin does not compare with the Hermitage in Leningrad, but it has a magnificent collection of French moderns. The date of the purchase is usually listed, and it is interesting to note that many were bought in the years immediately after the Second World War. In other words, while Zhdanov's purge of "cosmopolitanism" was at its height, curators of intelligence and good taste were quietly buying the works he damned and were, moreover, given state funds to do so.

Boris reiterated one theme endlessly: Girls! (Or, more precisely, Moscow girls!) The most beautiful girls in the world! And I must admit he found no shortage. When he telephoned them they came, and afterward he dismissed them. He divided women into two categories, which I did not quite follow. For Boris a girl was either "paradox" or "heterodox." In fact he seemed to find everything in life either paradox or heterodox.

Through Boris I met Vera. She was twenty-four and studied cinematography at the university—round-faced, pretty, blue-eyed, with wild dark hair falling over her eyes. "Vera is very orthodox," said Boris. "That's the paradox of it." And he rolled about with mirth at his sally. No one present ever laughed louder than Boris at his jokes. I suppose they lost something in translation.

"Whatever that may mean," said Vera, and I was no wiser than she. When I gave Vera some American lipstick and face powder, essential accessories for all travelers to Moscow, she burst into tears of emotion. She had no handkerchief so I gave her my packet of pocket Kleenex, which she also accepted with a kind of wonderment, giving a little scream of tearful laughter at the ingenious way the packet was opened by pulling a cord down the middle. As soon as her tears were dry she began busily to apply the lipstick. *"Schön,"* she said. *"Wunderschön."*

She told me, "I am so much in love with Boris, and Boris is in love with me. But the competition is too much—not for me but for Boris. The trouble is that Boris is in love with the whole world."

Vera's deepest passion was for the cinema and for her professor, the most important person in her life. (Russian students tend to float lovingly around their professors, like pilot fish around sharks, feeding on their wisdom.) She had gone with her professor to see films never shown publicly in the Soviet

Union, like *Bridge on the River Kwai*, *La Dolce Vita* and *High Noon*. Her professor spoke English, she said, and asked me to write the words of the bawdy British Army version of the *River Kwai* theme.

After some discussion on the influence of Antonioni, David Lean and Woody Allen on the cinema, Vera then got down to the essentials, the cinema she was *really* interested in. Would the Burton-Taylor marriage last? Was it true that Monica Vitti lived in sin with Antonioni? Was it true that so-and-so in Hollywood was a homosexual? Was Grace Kelly really happy as a princess living in Monte Carlo?

On our third meeting she showed me with delight a movie magazine she had acquired, apparently with a great deal of difficulty, and she seemed to expect me to be as impressed with it as she was. It was a wretched thing, published in East Berlin. I said, "I shall buy a subscription for you and your professor to *Cahiers du Cinéma* from Paris, and *Films and Filming* from London."

"Oh," said Vera, doubtfully. "I'm not so sure about that at all."

"Why?" I asked, intrigued. "Surely there would be no difficulty about your receiving it?"

"I don't know," she said. "Ask somebody. I cannot tell you."

She obviously wanted to change the subject. A few days later I suggested it again, and again she hedged, so I let the matter drop. I had already given her a copy of *Paris-Match*, which she read avidly, with particular attention to the ads, but it was clear that the idea of a subscription to any Western magazine was disturbing to her.

Subsequently I acquired the private handbook issued by the U.S. Embassy to newly arrived personnel. It says, "Unauthorized distribution of foreign literature is not permitted although the occasional gift of a foreign publication to a Soviet citizen who has indicated willingness to accept it is permissible."

The inhibition is not restricted to the Soviet Union. It also applies in sophisticated Poland. Even while writing this book, after my traumatic arrival in Warsaw described earlier, I made a similar offer to a woman lawyer I knew. "Do you want to get me in jail?" she asked.

My high respect for Boris's taste plummeted when he brought Sonia to the restaurant. Sonia was much more in the muscle-bound Muscovite tradition that Westerners have come to expect. She was—let me be a gentleman about it—a big woman, about twenty-seven years old, and she worked as a chemist in a research laboratory on the outskirts of the city. She could have been quite attractive in a Juno-esque way, but her hair had been dyed a ginger color of sorts, and the black showed at the roots. Her lipstick made her look as if she were bleeding. The most one could say about her teeth was that they looked strong. The top of her dark-green woolen dress sparkled with beads.

Speaking German, we trod our way through a verbal minefield into an area of agreed mutual hostility. She asked me politely enough about New York—and its crime. But I noticed, as I mentioned the charm of Greenwich Village and the splendors of Fifth Avenue, that she was pursing her lips in a muscular contortion which indicated without ambivalence, "Who do you think you are kidding, sweetheart?"

What she said was, "I have read differently, in the Soviet press."

I switched to London. This exasperated her. She cut me short, as though my insults to her intelligence had gone on far too long. "I am sorry," she said, "but I suspect you have never even been to London. Everybody knows that London is poor and dirty, and that people die in the toxic fumes of the fog. The food is rationed, and everybody has to go to bed at night because it is raining and they are so cold, and they have to sleep four in a bed."

I thought of the sun shining on London (usually on a Wednesday afternoon in July, and occasionally even in August).

It was the kind of remark Westerners never really believe Muscovites ever really make. I thought of trendy King's Road and the Portobello Road, and the traffic jams of Jags and Porsches. I forbore to reply.

Boris kissed his palm and tossed it into the air. "Ah, Moscow girls!" he cried, and bellowed to the waiter for more vodka.

Sonia softened slightly. "Look at Boris with his handsome new tie," she said. "He is also wearing his white shirt. He has only one, and he keeps it for May Day and all public celebrations."

I decided on a slight jab. "I am not surprised he only has one shirt. I was looking at the prices in GUM this morning, and shirts are twice the price they are in New York."

Sonia studied her beet-red fingernails. "The question of quality comes into it also," she said quietly.

"Just so," I said, but I don't quite know who won the encounter.

This obscurantism is not restricted to unfortunate Russians who have no opportunity to know any better. It can be a deliberate intellectual forgery, by people who know the truth. In the previous chapter, we find Dr. Olga deriding the French cuisine in comparison to the Russian cuisine. I offer now a much more flagrant, almost unbelievable example, from Ludmilla Sovolyeva, who played Natasha in Sergey Bondarchuk's epic *War and Peace*. Sovolyeva, a dancer in the Kirov Ballet, had been picked by Bondarchuk because of her resemblance to Audrey Hepburn in the Hollywood version.

In the fall of 1968 I attended the Broadway premiere of the film. In Russia the original ran for eight hours. The American version was cut to six and, for the premiere, was divided into two parts. The first began at two in the afternoon. At five one went home to change into evening dress, and the second half resumed at seven. Afterward there was a gala dinner with caviar and Russian vodka at the Americana Hotel, attended by all the Russian stars of the film. Bondarchuk himself was there; he had produced and directed the film, and miscast himself as Pierre.

At some point in the evening a harassed organizer came over to our table and said, "Does anybody here speak French? Bondarchuk is talking business with some Hollywood distributor, and Ludmilla is sitting alone. She can't speak English, and she is bored to death."

This was an opportunity not to be missed. I leaped to my feet and was led to the table of honor, where I was introduced to Ludmilla Sovolyeva. There followed some aimless small talk. Were the cuts in the film very important? Quite a lot. Where was Miss Sovolyeva staying? The Waldorf Towers. Did she enjoy it there?

At this Miss Sovolyeva sniffed disdainfully. "It's all right. It is not as good as Moscow hotels, of course."

I made my excuses as quickly as I could and fled back to my table with a mind that reeled.

Back to Moscow and Boris. The next girl he telephoned to "come and meet the Western writer" was Ilse, who was short, pert and wore her hair in rather silly bangs on her forehead. When she arrived Boris and I were sitting in the restaurant of the Metropole, both slightly drunk, and Boris was sketching a very clever, highly blasphemous Christ on the Cross. Ilse sat down, took the sheet of paper and tore it to bits. Boris smiled and looked philosophically into space, like a husband waiting to be henpecked. Ilse scowled at him.

"Why did you do that?" I said, really angry. "I was going to ask him for it."

"I disapprove of it," Ilse replied calmly, "so that's that."

"Surely not on moral grounds?"

"No. I am not a moralist. I have my reasons, and I am not sorry."

Boris smiled cheerfully and said nothing. I persisted. "Tell me why you tore up the drawing. As far as I'm concerned, it's vandalism "

Ilse said, "I have seen him draw the same thing so many times. It is Boris's fundamental doodle. Is he an artist or is he a copyist?"

"Relevant," said Boris. "Not necessarily accurate, but relevant. Paradox."

Ilse turned her back on him with a frown, and announced to me after belated introductions, "I am from Riga. I don't suppose you have ever heard of Riga. I never met a foreigner who did."

"Indeed I have heard of Riga. It is the capital of Latvia, one of the three Baltic states, along with Estonia and Lithuania."

"Good," she said. She looked at me thoughtfully for some time, as though hesitating to ask the question in her mind. At one moment it seemed as though she were about to abandon the subject altogether, but then she said, "What do you know about Riga? And Latvia?"

Now it was my turn to hesitate, but I too plunged in. "It was an independent democratic state until 1940. It was then annexed by the Soviet Union, with the other two Baltic states, and it has been a Russian colony ever since. Am I correct?"

Ilse beamed like a schoolteacher whose pet pupil has just answered a complex question. "Ex-*actly!*" she said. "Ex-*actly!*"

Boris was not too happy about the direction of the conversation, and started to draw Jesus again with a certain defiance. "We Russians are lousy soldiers," he said, apropos of nothing very much.

"What?" I asked.

He said, "I don't mean to say we are not good soldiers. I don't give a damn one way or the other. We don't care whether we are good soldiers or bad soldiers. We just don't like playing soldiers."

Now that we had settled the fate of Latvia, we switched to Italy. Ilse had been with Galina to see *Dolce Vita*, and could think only of seeing Rome. "Why don't you work at it?" I said. "Apply for a visa, get a student-exchange scholarship."

Ilse, with justice, looked at me as if I had disappointed her. "I should not like you to leave the Soviet Union," she said sweetly, "under the impression that this is a free country."

I would mislead the reader, however, if I give the impression that Moscow is full of pretty girls. Vera, Asya and, to a lesser extent, Ilse, are girls who make what they can out of the miserable tools the state puts at their disposal. One long-term Moscow hand goes so far as to say that there is not a single woman in Moscow, including the movie stars, that a sophisticated Westerner would call really well dressed from head to toe.

Also, the girls I have mentioned are young. The age group that ranges from about forty up is still heavily touched with standards of which Stalin would have approved. Too many Moscow women still go to smart restaurants thinking that they should look like Theda Bara or Vilma Banky. Their lips are painted in grotesque Cupid's bows. They wear dresses of satin or velvet, to which they add long gloves, and may top it off with a feather boa. After dancing with their escorts they are quite likely to drop a curtsy.

It is so difficult for them that it makes one weep. One has to blame the callousness of the leaders in the Kremlin, not necessarily the Communist system itself, because one sees plenty of smart women in Budapest and Prague. In Warsaw the styles were elegant indeed. At the Grand Theater I saw as many evening dresses and black ties as one would see normally at the Met or at Covent Garden.

The blame must be laid at the door of a long succession of drab Russian leaders, and their dumpy, ugly wives who look even worse when they tart themselves up to visit the West with their husbands. The beauty of John F. Kennedy made the Russians ashamed of Nikita Khrushchev, and the ugliness of Russian women in authority made the girls ashamed of themselves.

Style comes to the Russians in strange and unlikely ways. One is through Finnish television, the only Western television service which can be seen in the Soviet Union. The range is limited to Leningrad, Talinin and their environs. Nearly all European countries use women TV announcers, called, in French, *speakerines*. A Finnish *speakerine*, wearing a new dress, will be studied carefully in Leningrad, and her dress copied. Finns can also watch Leningrad television. Women throughout Finland wait with sardonic curiosity to see how long it will be before the *speakerine* in Leningrad appears in a copy of the same dress. The optimum time is one month, and, when it appears, there are cheers in the Helsinki studio. My source of information was one of the Finnish *speakerines* herself.

The Russian women are certainly trying. It is agonizing for them to realize how frumpish they appear in Western eyes. Their determination to do something about it deserves the most genuine praise and admiration when they come near to succeeding, and sympathy, not derision, when they fail.

11

The Young Men
of Moscow

Ten years ago the young Muscovite male was the most wretched urban specimen in Europe. He was whey-faced, undersexed and stunted. He hunched over heated radiators in cramped apartments, drinking vodka and tea with his girl friend, his mother, his father and an assembly of relatives as drab as he.

His face had a glutinous quality from eating too much fried and starchy food, the cuisine of a people to whom hunger was still a living memory. The compression of so many people in small airless rooms made him a prey to tuberculosis. The idea of a healthy walk in Gorky Park to feel the cold air on his cheeks would never have occurred to him. Admittedly, he beat the Germans in the Second World War, but, then, so did we.

Not the least repellent aspect of Stalin's personality was the total contempt in which he held young Russians. He sent them to their death with a profligacy that would have aroused the envy of even the French generals of the First World War. He cleared minefields by sending his young soldiers charging over them, and those taken prisoner were subsequently sent to Siberia in disgrace. They died in their millions with the word "Stalin" on their lips. Those who survived could rot. The kids not only smelled bad, they were given not the slightest incentive to smell any better.

To say that conditions have changed radically in the mid-

1970s would be to exaggerate. There is still a gaunt and prissy quality about many of Moscow's young men. They sit on park benches because they think sitting on grass is not *kulturny*. They have an excessive taste for ice cream, and they think it chic to eat chocolate éclairs.

If one loves the Russians, the changes in the young men fill one with "sympathie"—not sympathy, but warmth and a kind of compassion. The fellow tries so hard. In the last five or six years he has tended to a sort of old-fashioned dandyism. He will wear the kind of pointed, winkle-picker shoes that Italians wore fifteen years ago, if such precious items can be found. He affects a rather elegant drawl—the way, I suspect, Russians did before the Revolution. If he is from Leningrad he will probably describe himself as a Petersburgher. If he has the hard currency required at a hotel cocktail bar he will order gin or scotch, never vodka.

He is an agreeable chap and would like to be more agreeable still, but always the twin forces of shame and fear rise to build an impenetrable barrier. He is painfully aware that his clothes and ignorance of the current trends of the Western world make him a laughingstock to foreigners. If he strikes up a friendship with a Westerner, which he always longs to do, he will sooner or later be in trouble—with his professors, frequently his friends, and ultimately the police.

In winter I love to stand and watch the vast open-air swimming pool just outside the Kremlin walls on the banks of the River Moskva. The water, of course, is heated. On a freezing Moscow night, with snow falling out of the black skies, the steam rising from the pool gives it an almost hellish ambience.

It was not originally designed as a swimming pool. The site was intended for the world's tallest building, the Palace of the Soviets. Only after they had razed historic churches and some of the oldest sections of Moscow did the authorities find out that the clay subsoil would never support such a building. So it was left as a hole in the ground for years, until someone thought of making it a swimming pool.

I have often taken a swimsuit on my trips to Moscow, intending to apply myself to personal research, but when the crunch came I was too cowardly. It is a fantastic and impressive experience to stand hunched in fifteen thicknesses of cloth and watch beefy young Muscovites, in swimsuits no bigger than jockstraps, sporting in and out of the water. These healthy and comparatively uninhibited young men symbolize for me what Russians might yet become—ordinary people, thinking for themselves. They have made progress. They have never had to fear the knock of the secret police in the small hours of the night, or the ears of their neighbors against the wall for some indiscreet remark which would be immediately reported.

But outside, in the snow, stands the older generation, the living remnant of Stalin's paranoid Russia. I like to watch their faces, especially those in their forties and fifties. They were young during Stalin's last years of megalomania, and they helped sow the dragon's teeth. No Western generation gap compares with the generation gap in the Soviet Union.

They never learned how to swim, and they watch the swimmers with envy. Some show unconcealed resentment, even hate, and one can hear them muttering into the scarves that cover their noses and mouths. They, like the drinkers, miss the old days. Stalin at least kept them blinkered from the frightening world of ideas outside their borders. By the time the blinkers came off they had forgotten how to think.

They are not a unique phenomenon. They are quiet now, but so are the millions of Americans who backed Joseph McCarthy. That does not mean to say they don't miss him, or dream of his resurrection in another body. These Muscovites are the rudest to tourists. They wipe lipstick off their daughters' faces. They hate jazz, and in a restaurant will rise to remonstrate with youngsters whom they see letting their hair down.

They are a dying breed, and the young ones laugh at them. The youngsters pour out of the great universities with important degrees. They will not be shucked off by propaganda. They are almost pathetically hungry for new ideas and for everything

Western. Many read the *samizdat*, the underground literature, typed up with carbons and passed from hand to hand until they disintegrate. (I must add in the interests of accuracy that despite the heroic reputation of *samizdat* it publishes a great deal of pretentious rubbish as well as the forbidden masterpieces.)

They are still a little leery of Solzhenitsyn, and less tolerant of his political and religious eccentricities than the West is, but they revere Boris Pasternak. His grave at Peredelkino is never without flowers. They still look for intellectual guidance and courage to such aging whiz kids as Yevtushenko, Nekrassov and Voznessensky. I have not yet met any who knew—or at least admitted they knew—the works of poor Andrey Amalrik, who seems to get slung back into prison as soon as they let him out.

Jazz remains the umbilical cord that binds young Muscovites to the West. I have described my encounter with the Bolshoy jazz fans. Jazz is played in every restaurant every night, and often well. I commend the Café Molodyozhnoye at 41 Gorky Street, just beyond Mayakovsky Square, where there is a jam session every Friday night, and where is served perhaps the only good coffee in Moscow (tourists, stick to Russian tea). The waiters jive as they serve.

The hunger for the West, however, has fundamental limitations. The Stalinist religion, which directs all human energy toward the work norm, has left its inevitable blight on the young men of the capital—much more so in Moscow than in Leningrad, which is still what Peter the Great made it: a window on the West. The ordinary fellow, even the intelligent student, has not fully learned to understand the pleasures of human personality. The standard of literary, theatrical and art criticism is usually abysmal.

Under the Soviets, as under the tsars, people are nullified and neutralized by their initials, never their names. Writers, scientists, stage stars, politicians are without given names. Americans not only display their given names, they bare their souls with their middle initials, a practice almost unknown outside the United States. Occasionally they even add a hier-archical "Jr." or "III." Such flagrant indiscretion, such nomen-clatural nudism, is inconceivable to Russians, from J. V. Stalin and L. Brezhnev down.

We in the West tend to be hypnotized more by people than by ideas or philosophy. We are avid for memoirs and media revelations that tell all, for gossip columns, sporting giants, court trials, TV heroes.

The young Muscovite does not find it easy to talk about people as people. I was having a beer and a salami with a couple of architectural students in the beer hall of that crenellated monstrosity, the Ukraine Hotel, when I saw across the room a disintegrating old waiter whom I remembered talking to on my previous visit two years earlier.

"An interesting old chap," I said. "He went to Liverpool once before the First World War as a deck boy on a merchant ship; he even remembered the word 'Delly,' which Liverpudlians, and only Liverpudlians, call the Adelphi Hotel. In fact it was probably the only word in English he knew."

The students looked from the old man to me and back with open mouths. In a crescendo of incredulity, ending almost on a high C, they exclaimed, "What! You recognize a waiter!! You chatted with him!!! You *remember* him!!!" The clear implication was that I must have been wasting my time disastrously, when I should have been commuting between factory and museum. Western decadence revealed in the flesh.

It is always difficult to resist pulling Russian legs, particularly those of young Russians.

"Yes," I said, mild-eyed and blandly. "His name is Vol-odzye." It goes without saying I was lying; I hadn't a clue what the old boy's name was (though the rest was true). But it completed the disarray of my companions.

When they recovered they discussed architecture. Both young men were unexpectedly well informed. They wanted to know if New Yorkers considered the Guggenheim Museum to be a good example of the work of Frank Lloyd Wright, or did they consider it upset the rhythm of New York style. They were impressed by the Seagram Building and wanted to know what I thought of the Chicago tradition of architecture. Indeed, they knew much more than I.

My sense of mild malice was not altogether unappeased. I tried to bring the subject around to modern Moscow architecture, and particular the skyscrapers that stab the air like thistles in cut grass. Both shrugged my questions away as if I were insulting their intelligence, which in a way I was. Actually, I *like* the wedding-cake skyscrapers, such as Moscow University and the Foreign Office, and I even like Stalin's Palace of Culture in Warsaw. I can attest that they look better outside than in; inside the paint is flaking, the windows broken. Russians seem to take no pride in what does not belong to them; they leave it all to the state.

But then one of the boys burst out, "How can you read all those conflicting stories and opinions in your newspapers? How do you know what to believe?"

It was a tiny *cri de coeur*. One rarely gets into political argument in Moscow. This is an unspoken no-man's land respected by both sides. When one meets an agreeable person from "the other side" (of what?), neither wants the relationship to turn sour. But when a political tangle does occur, the ultradoctrinated Muscovite is a pushover. One would think that, with his monopolitical force-fed Communism, his armor would be impenetrable, and he would have the correct answer to everything. The opposite is true. The path he treads through the minefield of ideas is so narrow and so circumscribed that if he is compelled to make even half a turn he blows himself to bits.

I had an argument with a young man of twenty-five called Yuri, who declared himself by stating he was a graduate of the Komsomol, which vividly resembles our Boy Scouts because it differs so completely in every way. For a good half hour we verbally exchanged blow for blow. I was warming up. I did not realize that Yuri was sagging.

"Take the Berlin Wall," I said. "Put up by Ulbricht with the approval of your esteemed leader, Khrushchev (Yuri winced). "Before it went up 3 million East Germans had fled the Communist paradise." Yuri called me a liar.

"You won't believe me, Yuri," I said. "Even if I tell you I watched the process with my own eyes, as a foreign correspondent. Three thousand refugees arriving *every day* in West Berlin. But even if you don't believe me, I can scarcely invent 3 million people out of 17 million. Not only was the exodus witnessed by the entire world, but Ulbricht himself admitted it in a public speech to the East German Trades Unions on October 25, 1964." (Reader, I was lying in my teeth. As far as I know no such speech or admission was ever publicly made, on that or any other date, to trade unions or anyone else. But Communists regard statistics like that as the seal of accuracy.)

Yuri, as I said, had been hitting me hard, and I still did not realize that he was on the ropes. I waited for a counter to call my bluff, but it did not come. All Yuri could do was to stammer, "*Pravda* says nothing of this, so how can I tell?"

"Really? What does the word *Pravda* mean? Ah, yes, truth."

Now if anyone insulted *my* Holy Bible, I would have been annoyed and rushed with spirit to its defense. *Pravda* was Yuri's Bible. The raillery in my remark was too much for him. He got to his feet and flung out of the restaurant, keeping his face turned from the other diners. I don't know if he was in tears of anger or not. He was on his way, I guess, to seek consolation and reassurance from his seniors at the Komsomol. ("There, there, Yuri, don't get upset. The nasty foreigner will soon go away.")

The population of Moscow has jumped from a million to more than 5 million in thirty-five years. The City Fathers use this huge expansion as their excuse for the dreadful housing conditions. But it is only an excuse. Housing in Moscow has always been bad. Liam O'Flaherty, in his book *I Went to Moscow*, published in 1930, reported that he was invited to an apartment occupied by a high Soviet dignitary and his English wife—this being the period when it was considered rather smart by English and American intellectual women to marry into the Soviet Union. O'Flaherty wrote, "I was deeply impressed by the simplicity of their living quarters. Their home was like a council flat in the East End of London."

Political and social status is only comparative where housing is concerned. Correspondents constantly remind us that Andrey Sakharov, the nuclear physicist and Nobel Prize winner, lives with his family in two rooms. In 1965 Maya Plissetskaya, the greatest star of the Bolshoi Ballet, was living in a single room with her husband, Rodion Shchedrin, and sharing a kitchen and bathroom with eleven other families. Then, because her husband is a composer and needs a room to work in, they were awarded a four-room apartment.

To return to my subject of how young people make love, they can't do it in cars, because no one has a car. They cannot check into a hotel room without a permit. This tends to make the Moscow girl both wild and adventurous; a bachelor foreign correspondent living in a privileged diplomatic apartment on the Kutuzovsky Prospect or one of the other foreign compounds has no girl problem save that of surfeit.

One American correspondent, who had been seeking only to oblige the young ladies he was meeting, was called into the Soviet Press Office in the Foreign Ministry and ordered to stop corrupting young Moscow womanhood. "Who is corrupting whom?" the correspondent demanded, aggrieved. "I'm running away, not chasing. And in any case," he added, voicing a complaint about the double standard that was annoying many Westerners at the time, "you let the Arabs get away with anything. The girls merely have to tell the policeman on duty outside that they are seeing Arabs, and they are allowed to visit their apartments in droves."

The ministry official ignored the point and would not be budged from the theme. "If you want to go out with one Russian girl on a regular basis, we will raise no objection," he said. "And as far as Western girls living or visiting in Moscow are concerned, you can see as many as you like. But if you continue this promiscuity with Soviet girls, you will lose your accreditation to the Soviet Union and go out on your ass." And, as it happens, out he went not long afterward.

Such is the official Soviet line, which gives just one more illustration of why the job of a foreign correspondent is so much more difficult in Moscow than it is in, say, Paris or Bonn.

But a certain bohemianism is hovering, and the climate is becoming increasingly suitable for a splashdown. There exists in Moscow a leisured society which the Soviet Union acknowledges only when cornered, but which can be seen chatting for hours on end in the better restaurants and coffeehouses of the city—cafés like the gigantic Arbat, the Ailit or the more distant Yunost Hotel near Dynamo Stadium. What these elegant, often seemingly epicene people do for a living in such a harsh, demanding society it is difficult to say. The young men have their hair greased down like silent-movie stars; only a few wear it occidentally long. They smoke Western cigarettes. The girls are pretty, and their hair styles are only a year or two out of date by the standards of New York.

Some of them are people of artistic achievement: painters, sculptors, actors, with plenty of time on their hands, although writers and certain artists prefer to assemble in their union clubs rather than in public places.

Others are what the Soviet Union calls parasites—sons and daughters of generals or judges, often speaking in a nasal drawl and pretending to be Americans. These are the true spawn of the late Jan Rokotov. The elderly Party faithful form a perfect *bourgeoisie* against which to revolt. It is interesting, though not really surprising, to realize that these elders are Soviet conformists the way Archie Bunker is an American conformist and Alf Garnett an English conformist. They favor such things as overstuffed chairs, plush fringed tablecloths and beaded lampshades.

The children of these parents are the troublemakers of the

capital. They smash things, wreck their parents' cars and beat up the militia. In restaurants they behave in disorderly fashion—tourists can often see them in smart restaurants at night, the Arbat, the Roof Garden of the Hotel Moskva on Marx Prospect, the Rossiya. If they get so obstreperous that the police have to be called, they shout things like, "My father is a judge, and he will chop your nuts off if you lay a hand on me." The police then usually go away, gray-faced.

During the day they skip their studies and sit hour after hour over coffee. If they spot a Westerner they can become a royal pain in the neck. They promptly come over and sit down with him—one of the most charming features of Moscow life, the one way one often makes good friends with Muscovites, but not with this different breed of cat.

The first thing they do is show the labels on the inside of their suits, curious to know more of the pedigree. I have seen "Austin Reed of Regent Street," "Rogers Peet, New York," but more often some name unknown to me, originating in St. Louis, Dusseldorf, Zürich, once even Kyoto. I have seen button-down collar shirts unmistakably from the cutting room of the Madison Avenue Brothers, sometimes frayed at the cuffs and faded from much loving wash, always worn with pride. And invariably the question is put to one, as if it were of crucial importance:

"Smart? Elegant? Chic? Good shop?"

"Very elegant, *très* chic, *sehr hübsch*. Very good shop." They sigh with pleasure and smile triumphantly at their girl friends, as though saying, "I told you so."

So far they are harmless. But then the conversation begins to progress like this:

"You American? I spik ver' good American. Oh my aching back."

"Quite."

"I talk ver' good American, eh? You can say that again."

"Thank you, I'd rather not."

"Oh my aching back. You American? I talk good American,

baby, okay? I'm cat's pajamas. Raquel Welsh jiggyjig... Me gentleman. Prince. Fuck Komsomol.* Chic suit, eh...?"

This rewarding and illuminating monologue will continue ad nauseam, with the Westerner trapped by his desire not to offend.

There has to come a time when the young Muscovite insists on an apartment of his own. He does not ask for much, merely something beyond his wildest dreams: a single room, nine feet by twelve feet, a two-ring gas burner to cook coffee and sausages, a lavatory in which he can relax with a book, without worrying about people waiting outside and banging on the door. On the walls he will be able to hang a reproduction of a Klee or even a Warhol. On a table of his own he can keep a bottle of vodka, and some wine and beer. In his drawer he can keep a clandestine, disintegrating copy of *Playboy*. He can invite friends up to listen to Nashville music and have his girl stay the night without nosy neighbors knowing all about it.

When—and if—such dreams come true, before the Kremlin realizes it he will be almost like us.

---

* The Russian language carries no definite or indefinite article.

12

Yet Somehow They Know, They Know Even Now

> When your son is discontented in France, use my formula and say to him, "Go to Russia."
>
> —Marquis de Custine, 1839

> There is nothing like a stay in the U.S.S.R. to help us appreciate ... what we still enjoy in France, and sometimes abuse.
>
> —André Gide, 1935

> *Custine, a monarchist, went to Russia to admire the monarchy and returned a republican. Gide went to Moscow a Communist, and returned anti.*

It is hard to comprehend that Muscovites not only wade through *Pravda* and *Izvestia* but actually believe what they read in them. The four-page newspapers are displayed in glass cases on walls all over the city, and even in the bitterest of winter days one sees citizens stamping their feet and wiping the glass free of frost with their gloved hands to study the wisdom behind it. Well, some people read the London *Morning Star*, organ of the British Communist Party, but I never met a Fleet Street man who did.

When Boris Pasternak, author of *Dr. Zhivago*, died in official disgrace in 1960, the Soviet authorities suppressed the news and nothing appeared in any of the media. Yet hundreds of Muscovites, mostly young, traveled to Pasternak's village of Peredelkino on the day of his burial to pay their last respects. The question poses itself: how on earth did they know?

The answer is that they heard it in the Russian-language broadcasts of the B.B.C. World Service. It is almost impossible to exaggerate the importance of the B.B.C. World Service to the Russian intellectual. The Voice of America, Radio Free Europe and Radio Liberty come nowhere in comparative statistics. To us in the West the objective reporting of all news, good and bad, for and against, is so much a part of our life we never think about it. Is there any other way? But the Russian press and broadcasting service has still not reported Khrushchev's denunciation of Stalin in 1956.

Imagine what it means to switch on one's set to short wave and hear that Svetlana Stalin, daughter of the old rascal, has defected to the West, that Nureyev and then Makarova and then Baryshnikov have all defected from the Kirov Ballet, that Alexander Solzhenitsyn has been awarded the Nobel Prize and then kicked out of the country, that an Ilyushin jumbo jet has crashed at Leningrad Airport. None of this is reported inside Russia. Imagine further hearing in news bulletins that ink had been thrown at the then Prime Minister, Ted Heath, or that the House of Commons was debating the income of the Queen of England.

The B.B.C. World Service is legendary. Russian émigrés passing through London regularly look in on Bush House in the Strand to say hello to Anatole Maximovitch Goldberg, the senior broadcaster in the Russian language. They keep the Russian desk up to date on listenership within the Soviet Union. The fact is that the B.B.C.'s admirers in Russia form almost a Who's Who of the nation's scholarship. When Alexander Solzhenitsyn arrived in Switzerland after his expulsion from the Soviet Union in February 1974, he was forced to lock himself away against the onslaught of the world's press. The only journalist he would see was Janis Sapiets of the B.B.C., because Solzhenitsyn knew his name and voice. Solzhenitsyn told him he listened to the religious broadcasts, and that it was on the B.B.C. that he first heard of his Nobel Prize.

Zhores Medvedev, the Russian scientist, tells in his book *A Question of Madness* about being released from an insane asylum where the authorities had confined him for dissidence. The first thing he did on returning home was to switch on the B.B.C., and there heard the announcement of his release. The news was followed by a commentary from Maurice Latey, analyzing the predicament of dissident intellectuals in the Soviet Union and the methods used to silence them.

Western broadcasts are sporadically jammed. *Pravda* has called objectivity of news "the secret weapon of capitalism." To jam the broadcasts Russia and her satellites use no fewer than three thousand transmitters, which cost more than $200 million to install and $80 million annually to maintain. This is more than the Soviet Union spends on its domestic radio service, and nearly three times as much as the British government gives the B.B.C. to run its external services. There could be no greater concession of intellectual defeat, or greater compliment to the B.B.C. as the Soviet Union's principal intellectual adversary.... No, there is a greater compliment yet. During the fiercest jamming the Russians keep one frequency open for monitoring. The Russian intelligence authorities themselves want to know what is going on in the world!

Anatole Goldberg, chief commentator of the East European Service, is in a small, specialized way something of a cult figure in the Soviet Union. He was born in Leningrad in 1910; grew up in Germany; left there as a Jewish refugee in 1936; and joined the B.B.C. in 1939. He told me a delightful story that happened when George Brown went to Russia as Foreign Secretary. Goldberg went along as interpreter. Their aircraft was obliged to land in Leningrad on account of bad weather conditions, and the journey had to be completed by train. Goldberg, at Brown's request, called the stationmaster to thank him for his courtesy. At the mention of Goldberg's name the stationmaster looked startled, looked at his watch and said, "But Anatoly Maximovitch, you should be broadcasting on the B.B.C. in a quarter of an hour."

An émigré in London, making the almost ritual call on Goldberg, told him another story. A master of ceremonies in Kiev was introducing to a lecture audience a writer called Anatole Maximovitch. The M.C., somewhat distrait, announced him as "Anatoly Maximovitch Goldberg." There was a moment of surprised silence, and then a yell of laughter from what was evidently an extremely well informed audience. Soviet Union-wise, that's fame.

In 1974 an independent, confidential poll taken of Russian émigrés in Israel and elsewhere found that the Voice of America in its seventy-four hours of broadcasts to the Soviet Union held only a 3 percent edge in listening time over the B.B.C. with its thirty-one hours of broadcasting time. Many of those said they listened to the Voice of America only because they could not get the B.B.C. Radio Liberty, broadcasting round the clock, fared poorly. Russians intelligent enough to listen to Western broadcasts know that the Voice of America is run as a government agency. They know that Radio Liberty and Radio Free Europe have been financed in the past by the C.I.A. And they know that the B.B.C. is independent and objective. The B.B.C. is the last abiding legacy of the British Empire, and it undoubtedly rules the waves.

If Russians know what is happening in the West they also know only too well what Westerners are up to in Russia. Some years ago, shortly before her death, I had the privilege of meeting Mme. Eisenstein (pronounced *Ayzenshtayn* in Russian), the widow of Serzey Eisenstein, the great Russian film director. She lived with a lady companion in a minuscule two-room apartment in Moscow. The inevitable Novosti girl was present, and there was scarcely room for the four of us in the living room.

Although Mme. Eisenstein had never been farther abroad than Poland, she spoke fluent English. She revealed that she had a sister living on Riverside Drive in New York and asked if I would take a parcel of presents to her small nieces. I was more than happy to oblige. The parcel contained the usual Russian toys—round wooden dolls containing identical but smaller dolls, containing smaller dolls in turn.

Miss Novosti and I paid our farewells; I took the parcel to my room in the Leningradskaya Hotel and dumped it with my own purchases and piles of personal belongings on the spare twin bed. I thought no more about it. My visit to Moscow had another week to run. When it became time to pack and leave for the airport, the parcel was not there.

Admittedly, it is against Soviet law to take letters and packages out of the country for others, but neither Mme. Eisenstein nor I had thought of that. My friendly Novosti girl had clearly reported the dastardly conspiracy, and someone had entered my room and taken it. There was no way I could contact Mme. Eisenstein, and as her sister's name and address were on the purloined package I could not—despite considerable effort on my part—trace her on Riverside Drive to say what had happened. So no one ever knew.

13

So You Are Going to Moscow Anyway

The traveler to Russia should be provided with a pillow or air cushion, linen sheets (useful on long railways journeys and in provincial hotels), towels, a coverlet or rug, a small india-rubber bath, and some insect powder.

—*Baedeker*, 1914

If the western tourist does not like paying thirty-five times as much as the native for his hotel room (in Moscow) he can always stay home.

—GEORGE FEIFER, *Our Motherland*, 1973

When I was last in Moscow some three thousand Canadians had taken over the city for the world championship hockey battle with the Soviet Union. (The Russians won.) They were scarcely Canada's finest and were mostly undistinguished in personal presentation. Some of the ladies appeared in public rooms with their hair in curlers. Several of the gentlemen dined showing their galluses. Red maple leaves were so numerous that they seemed to turn Moscow into an autumnal forest. The Canadian bravos did a brisk and illegal trade in selling their clothes to young Muscovites, pocketing a hundred dollars and more for blue jeans. To most Westerners the death penalty for black market crime seems a heavy penalty for buying an Eaton's shirt. But young Russians continue to take the risk.

One might be excused for thinking that such a mass invasion would overwhelm the Muscovites. Galluses or no galluses, they were all better dressed than the locals. Their noisiness and ebullience in the streets made a staggering contrast to the somber deportment of the natives. But Moscow took the Canadian invasion as it takes everything else. It is a city that cannot be fazed or discomposed. A squall of rain can make New York fall flat on its face. Queen Elizabeth can turn London into an impenetrable traffic jam simply by crossing the road to make her speech to Parliament. Insoluble chaos is part of the way of life of Rome and Paris. Not Moscow.

Moscow has played host to countless influxes of outsiders for a thousand years, starting with Ghengis Khan and his Mongols. Moscow was still there a few hundred years later when the Mongols got onto their ponies and rode back to Mongolia. Moscow has put up with agricultural delegations, later sweeping away the cow dung that fell from the delegates' boots; international film festivals, which Soviet films always seemed to win by unanimous decision; prize-winning coal miners with red tin medals on their homemade suits.

It has listened with incredulous disinterest to Angela Davis. It has put up with Elizabeth Taylor and Richard Burton by not noticing them, with Italian automobile manufacturers wearing the snappiest suits on earth and Siberian farmers with shoulder padding that could cushion a sofa. It has received African tribal delegations wearing robes and carrying fly swatters, with their wives strolling along the corridors with their breasts bare.

It has kept its cool while Cuban delegations played mariachis in their rooms after midnight and made passes at the chambermaids in the morning. It has accommodated English defectors, Canadian Unitarians, Cambodian refugees, Isadora Duncan, Bernard Shaw and Lady Astor. It has kept a straight face listening to the "Red Dean" of Canterbury, which was more than Robert Spivak was able to do on *Meet the Press*.

Moscow treats all its visiting hordes alike, without consideration of race, creed, color or even politics. It treats them without consideration, period. No, it treats blacks rather worse, to be accurate, because Russians are without exception racist. All visitors are treated with rudeness, indifference, disinterest, ignorance and, not infrequently, with open hostility and resentment.

And if you rile the Muscovites severely enough, they will deprive you of a place to stay by simply burning the entire city down and then composing overtures about it, as they did with Napoleon in 1812.

I have mentioned the Western sport of people-watching in Moscow, the pleasure the foreign correspondents take in observing the antics of the city's kooks and eccentrics. Vice is definitely not versa (with exceptions such as I will bring up in my concluding chapter). Muscovites have troubles of their own and just don't care. The British author James Kirkup, aware that Russian poets are in the habit of giving their poetry recitals in Mayakovsky Square, decided on an impulse to give a poetry recital of his own. He clambered up on the high plinth which holds the giant statue of Mayakovsky, and began to declaim his own works. Passersby took not the slightest notice of him.

After half an hour, in desperation, he switched to lyrics in Japanese. Still nobody turned to look at him. In the end a police constable approached, urged him to get down, accompanied him to his hotel and suggested he go to bed.

A similar compulsion happened to me once, with exactly the same reaction. The winter was one of the bitterest in memory, and I was staying at the National. To go from the National to the Central Telegraph Office, one turns left and left again into Gorky Street, with about a hundred yards to go. I decided to do it without coat or hat, in just a rather smart suit made by Doug Hayward of Mount Street, Mayfair. I left the hotel and made my trek. Same reaction as with Kirkup. Muscovites, their cheeks purple, their earflaps flapping, coated, scarved, hurried past me as though I weren't there.

The paradox lies in the fact that the same Russians, outside of their work hours, are among the most warm-hearted and hospitable people in the world. Cold climates are always conducive to hospitality, and the Russians actually take pride in admitting that they have the harshest climate in the world. The stranger invited to Russian homes reels under the weight of food and drink, and gifts as lavish as the hosts possess are pulled from mantelpieces or chests of drawers.

There will be laughter, noise, philosophical dissertations about man and his relationship to God, arguments on the best temperature in which to cook a chicken tabaka or the proper size of blini. There will be several not so covert cracks at the régime in the Kremlin. The stranger's departure will require at least three people to help him on with his coat and hat, and will be the signal for bear hugs, tears, declarations of undying friendship, promises to exchange letters, and wet kisses on the mouth.

These are the same people who, at work, assume a rudeness that almost reaches Parisian levels, and frequently succeeds; it all depends on which kind of rudeness you have the greater tolerance for: the Parisian stiletto or the Muscovite bludgeon. Some experts say the Moscow rudeness stems from the drabness of the work environment; the shoddiness of the materials in which the Russians are dealing; the complete absence of initiative or ambition; the suspicion of every man for his neighbor at work and at home. For people with so few luxuries and rights, the luxury and right to refuse to extend the slightest service or courtesy to others is not one to be given up lightly. Furthermore, it is almost impossible for anyone to be fired from his job, except for really grave offenses, like scrawling "Lenin was a soppy sod" with an aerosol spray gun along a Kremlin wall.

Like Parisians, Muscovites inflict their bile on each other as well as on strangers. The general, apathetic indifference often bursts into flaming rows on buses and in shopping queues. Perfect strangers feel free to join in and arbitrate or take sides. If no words are exchanged, loathing is expressed with a uniquely Russian shrug, unlike anything in the vast Italian repertoire of gestures. It is a flick of the shoulder which is an expression of contempt, a shrug of utter rejection.

Joseph Alsop, the American columnist, in one of his marvelously characteristic throwaway lines, established what I always think of as "Alsop's Law." Alsop's Law holds that a traveler to distant lands can always make a sound rule-of-thumb judgment on any country by studying its priorities—what it considers essential to do well, and what not to bother with. He noted that while all of the millions of Communist Chinese dressed identically in drab blue uniforms and flat blue caps, their cuisine was superb in its variety. He found the service in restaurants and factory cafeterias courteous and efficient, the napery spotless, and the chopsticks often of ivory.

In the Soviet Union, on the other hand, Alsop continues, there are scarcely half a dozen restaurants in the entire country where one can get a decent meal, reasonably served. There is not a single building from Leningrad to Vladivostock designed for business offices. Western banks, corporations and airlines operate out of rented suites in hotels, and foreign correspondents work in their apartments. No Russian with the slightest sense of taste would ever buy a Russian suit if he could possibly get his hands on a foreign suit.

(Americans will recall the dreadful pale-blue suit worn by Leonid Brezhnev when he addressed the people of the United States on television. The lapels belonged to something else altogether, the rest bulged and tucked in all the wrong places; one would scour every discount house in America and fail to find anything so shoddily made. Two years later he was still wearing the same suit to greet visiting dignitaries. We have not departed in any way from Alsop's Law: the priorities of the top man in the Soviet Union were elsewhere.)

Mr. Alsop resumes: on the other hand, the space achievements of the Soviet Union are magnificent, the Soviet Armed Forces are more powerful than those of the United States, the Russian Navy is probably the best in the world, and the nation's espionage networks, secret police and organization for the suppression of public protest are the envy of their counterparts everywhere. It is a simple question of priority, and those are areas of human endeavor which the régime considers the more important.

Moscow today is one of the world's major tourist capitals. The Soviet Union is far easier for a visitor to enter than the United States. Visas are easier and quicker to get. At Moscow Airport there is no customs inspection whatever (European visitors to the United States are appalled at the slowness of the immigration routine and the callous way American customs officers open every bag and finger through private belongings). At ports of entry into the Soviet Union the only form that has to be filled is a currency declaration. After clearance a taxi takes the tourist to his hotel without charge.

The Communist system is such that it has been able to resist worldwide inflation—the authorities boast that the price of bread has not risen since the war. Because Moscow has always preferred delegations to ordinary people, it can cope more efficiently with package tours than any other country except for, perhaps, Spain. At the time of writing this book, Pan American World Airways in conjunction with Aeroflot, the Soviet airline, offers a one-week package tour for $539. This includes round-trip transportation, hotel room and private bath for seven nights, three meals a day, daily sightseeing, theater performances in Moscow and Leningrad, gala dinner at a special restaurant, overnight excursion to the old Russian city of Kalinin, with all taxes, tips and service charges included.

This is the kind of thing the Russians do well. What it means is, it sticks the tourists where it wants them, bids them eat what is put on the plate before them and guides them where it wants them to go. Individuals are too much trouble. They tend to be nosy, get lost in the wrong places and occasionally wander, under escort, into the Lubyanka.

To understand Moscow's expansion and its significance to

prospective tourists, the clearest parallel is to consider the expansion of sport in the United States. Twenty years ago the United States had sixteen baseball teams. College football consumed a couple of months in the winter, climaxed by the Bowl games. Ice hockey was played by émigré Canadians in four American cities and two Canadian cities. That, more or less, was the sum of mass enthusiasm. Today it is all but impossible to follow the baseball, football, basketball, hockey and tennis mutations and expansions. There is not enough human talent to go round, or animal energy to satisfy public demand. All there is is money and spectators in abundance. The New York Mets, before their glory year of 1969, were amazingly awful to watch, but they filled the stadium.

A parallel situation pertains in Moscow today. In the early days of tourism to the Soviet Union, when Nikita Khrushchev was beginning to lift Stalin's curtain against foreigners, a few brave tourists, hearts beating in delicious dread and awful anticipation, ventured into the city. Every experience, good and bad, was exciting, from rush hour in the palatial Metro stations to eating ice cream at GUM, to the appalling service in the restaurants, to the majesty of the Bolshoi.

In the years since, millions of Western visitors have come to the Soviet Union. Not only has the service not improved, it has become worse. Here we return to the Alsop Law on priorities. Such Soviet catering experts who were sent to the West to study the hotel and restaurant business had their priorities well in mind, and they were not the priorities that would occur to us. As I have suggested earlier, even at best the hotel administrators are not among the proudest of Soviet society. On the contrary, they belong among the lowest in the Soviet social hierarchy. They would not have entered the business in the first place if they had been capable of anything else.

Thus, with no dedication whatever to higher standards of service and with an actual ideological revulsion against serving their fellow men on a master-servant basis, they are, more than most, concerned with one thing only—money. They visited the West; they studied the hotel and catering systems, and they absorbed their own lessons. The question of service and catering never entered into it. What they sought were the methods by which they could extract the maximum of foreign currency out of the visiting suckers. The lessons boiled down to two of the shortest words in the English language:

The TIP!

And—in lower case—the gyp.

Moscow has become the clip city of the civilized world, carried on as deliberate government policy from the highest echelons of the Intourist organization down to the smallest porter in the hotel. In its blatancy it even has a certain lunatic charm. Try to point out to them the error of their ways, and they would not know what on earth you were talking about. Surely, *tovarishch*, this is the way it is done in America! Don't you want to be made to feel at home?

I hereby give the prospective traveler to the Soviet Union not one but several examples and suggestions on how to beat the bums, because it hurts one to see so many well-meaning people visiting the Soviet Union for the worthiest of purposes getting so blatantly and sneeringly cheated. The gratuity mania, the service charges, the hustling and all the other little extras do not make Moscow a less exciting city. But nobody enjoys being made a patsy, and to do so has become Soviet policy at all levels, from détente, battleships, and criminal grain deals to tourism. Alexander Solzhenitsyn, Professor Sakharov, Medvedev, Mao Tsetung, and the others go around, as all honest men would do, shouting, "Don't tip the sonsofbitches! It's a ripoff!" But Nixon, Ford and Kissinger don't listen, any more than theater tourists on Broadway listen when they are warned not to drop coins into the collection boxes of lady panhandlers during intermission.

The process in the Russian tourist industry is identical. Earlier I quoted from the *Handbook of Foreign Tourism in the U.S.S.R.* Edited by one V. E. Ivanov, it leaves nothing out. It tells what restaurant waitresses must wear and even gives a list of state secrets which must not be mentioned in front of foreign visitors.

Among many other things it stipulates the distinctions between the money and the social standings of various foreign countries. The Socialist bloc is not at all solid. East Germans—although they are certainly unaware of the fact—are charged more than Poles or Bulgarians. No Mongolian of any rank is to be allowed first-class accommodation in Soviet hotels. Yugoslavs must pay in dollars (or presumably other West European currency).

The book tells how Intourist officials should explain certain misconceptions, despite what it says in the travel and propaganda brochures. For example, visitors from the West must pay for any medical service they receive. Yes, yes, the Soviet Union does have a free medical system, the envy of the world. But the system does not extend to visiting capitalists.

If the traveler's bag is lost or stolen from an Intourist hotel, the rules of the handbook specify that reimbursement, once the value is agreed, "is to be paid in Soviet rubles only." This chutzpah positively takes the breath away. Outside the Soviet Union the ruble could not even buy tsarist railroad stocks. The rubles cannot be changed or exported, and of course the rubbish on sale in Moscow stores can scarcely even be described. The traveler would not be able to buy a razor blade that would cut or a cake of soap that would make suds. Perhaps only Sid Caesar and Imogene Coca could do justice to the concept of two American tourists refurbishing their wardrobe in GUM.

All this is official government policy. Switch now to the lower-echelon gyps. The bar of the Rossiya Hotel is the nearest thing Moscow possesses to an up-to-date American cocktail bar. The décor is modern, and the view through the vast plate-glass windows is magnificent. The price of, say, a vodka and tonic—a very *small* measure of vodka by American standards—is $1.50 at the time of writing (and bet your boots it will be double when the Moscow Olympics are held).

The visitor puts down two dollars, drinks, looks at the

passing scene and the views out of the vast windows. If he is alert—and one often isn't when on holiday—he will notice after a while that no change has been proffered. He will draw the bartender's attention to this omission. There will be no apology or expression of contrition. At best the bartender may utter a slight cluck at his forgetfulness and produce the change. Moscow bartenders would never even think of remembering customers' faces, so the process is repeated every time with the same people, as though it were perfectly natural.

Similar practices have been observed, of course, in the West, though usually rather more subtly. But Moscow offers a really intriguing variation on the theme, which can not only be counterproductive to the operators but can provide some amusement to the visitor. Frustrating the knavish tricks of bartenders and sales clerks trying to steal one's money can add to the honest pleasures of the holiday itself.

The gyp is based on the rule that purchases must be made at Berioska stores and international bars in hard currency. *Any* hard currency. Now read on.

Let us suppose a tourist buys a lacquer box for $7.75, and presents a $10 bill. He will *never* get $2.25 in change. He will get perhaps $1.50, and the rest in a jumble of other currencies. He protests. He is then told that there is no more American money left in the till. "But why worry?—the remaining seventy-five cents is good for other purchases in Moscow." The presumption is that the tourist will shrug and leave the unwanted coins behind.

I hold that one is never made cheap by refusing to knuckle under to con artists. They are dealing in pennies, but so are we. It is important for future tourists to know what they are in for and make a game of it. A tourist buys a drink, and expects seventy-five cents in change from the bartender. He will get a quarter and the rest in incomprehensible coins. He says, "I don't want this money. It is useless to me."

The bartender replies, indifferently, "There's no more Amer-

ican change. I will give you South African rands." The tourist
will quickly learn that the change is always in obscure money
from countries he is not likely to visit: Japanese yen, Australian
cents, Norwegian crowns. These are kept as the bartender's
reserve. He never offers German pfennigs, English pence or
French centimes.

The argument resumes. "I don't want African rands."

"I don't have any more American currency."

The bartender wants his seventy-five cents. The tourist with
guts will not let him have it. It could be he is flying from
Moscow to Paris. "I'll take the rest in French money."

This is a good move. It means the bartender, teeth gnashing,
is obliged to return to his abacus, and work out a fresh rate of
exchange. Perspiration pours from his brow. His temper shreds.
But he still won't give in without a fight. He returns with fifty
cents in centimes and the balance in New Zealand money.

"I don't want this. New Zealand, I am afraid, is not in my
direction."

"I have no more French money," the liar says.

One now insists on the final quarter in Italian lire or English
pence. Fifteen cents arrives in English money and the final dime
in Danish øre. The eyes by now have become pleading. The
bartender almost whimpers, Surely, *tovarishch*, buddy, you can
spare an øre?

Not on your nelly you can't, not to these chiselers. Two
courses are open for complete and final moral victory. One can
insist on the remaining dime in German pfennigs or pocket the
Danish coin. The important thing is that it is not to go into the
pocket of this bastard. On one's next visit to an operating
church, one can pop it into the offertory box. There it will be
appreciated, and one can enjoy the feeling, especially agreeable
in this atheist society, of performing a Christian service.

Just outside the village of Saltikova, about twenty miles from
Moscow, a new night club called the Rus has been opened. Taxi
drivers and waiters push the Rus, and so does Intourist and the

chauffeurs of high government bureaucrats who moonlight by running their official Chaikas as taxis. There are pretty girls at the Rus. They are also friendly. They will be happy to accept a glass of Soviet champagne and will smatter in English or German. The waiter, apparently schooled along the Place Pigalle in Montmartre, produces a bottle. Caviar is supplied, unasked. The gullible client believes that this may be part of the standard service. Anyway, it would be ungallant to question the waiter in front of the girl, and the waiter does not speak English anyway.

At about two in the morning—my source for all this is not personal research but reports from the walking-wounded survivors—the girl's "husband" appears, looking surprised and hostile. His suspicions are soothed by being offered a glass of champagne. When the tourist asks for another glass the waiter obliges by presenting another bottle and more caviar. The "husband" takes the girl home. The tourist, to his astonishment, finds the taxi driver, or Brezhnev's chauffeur mentioned earlier, still waiting for him. He had waved the fellow away earlier, after his offer of money had been acknowledged with a shake of the head. The innocent tourist thought it an example of Russian good nature. But no, the tourist pays for the round trip, plus the hours of waiting time.

Some of the Canadian ice hockey enthusiasts mentioned earlier reported being ripped off at the Rus for $120 to $200.

I did not consider my duty to my reader sufficient to check this out personally, and I was leaving Moscow anyway the following day. But from Paris I wrote to a correspondent who is still serving there. He replied:

I have not been there myself; I'm avoiding it studiously. Pan Am gave a party there over Christmas, and I have details from a friend who attended. He said the interior and décor were okay—Russian rustic, and the atmosphere is cheerful. It has the usual problems of Russian service. They arrived by chartered bus and had reservations. But they had to wait outside on a snowy midwinter night for fifteen minutes before the staff would open up (about 6 P.M.). There was a passable soup, then the usual zakuski (minuscule caviar, minuscule sturgeon, plenty of cucumber and tomatoes), then a passable mushroom julienne. The main course was inedible and indefinable, some sort of meat of dubious origin. The liquor ration was not overly generous. But the band was good: our friends danced until eleven. Then the band packed up for an hour "because we have to play from midnight until three." As our friends were leaving the heavy mob started to arrive; drunken Georgians with expensive-looking girls.

The Georgians had bad luck, though, because as the Pan Am party left the Pan Am bus driver, apparently as tipsy as the rest, went into a ditch, knocked down a power pole and plunged the Rus into darkness, ending the entertainment for the night. The Pan Am crowd gamely shoved at the bus for two hours, then gave up and walked two miles through the snow to the nearest station. The highway police came up at one stage, took one look at the plight of the bus and drove hastily away without offering to help. A typical Moscow evening out! As Pan Am paid, our friends did not know what the tab came to. My own experiences with similar places suggests it was an absolute basic minimum of twenty-five dollars each.

Or perhaps I can be more precise, by quoting a parallel establishment, the Archangelskoye, a new, glass-box-type place. As none of the main dishes looked edible, we had soup; zakuski, of course; no main course at all; ice cream; one bottle of vodka between four, and one bottle of white wine. The check: 65 rubles, i.e., about $90. It has had a lot of official publicity—as indeed has had the Rus—and some people like it. Kosygin apparently didn't. The story goes that he went there for an official weekend banquet last summer, was so angered by the food he ordered everyone sacked and sent to Siberia. Next day a few heavies came out and fired everybody on the spot, from manager to busboy.

Daniel Yergin, a research fellow at Harvard, reported in *The New York Times* his adventures in renting a car to drive from Moscow to Leningrad. He hired it for three days and discovered later on that he had actually paid in advance for eight days, and there would be no refund on the money. He sat himself at the driver's wheel, and found the driver's seat immovably tilted at 30 degrees, ensuring a permanent backache for the entire trip. He pulled open the ashtray, and found it crammed to the tip with stubs. He checked his gas tank. He found it as empty as the ashtray was full.

He made the trip as planned and kept the car for five days, figuring that as he had paid for eight, he was getting a couple of days at least for free. The simpleton did not know his Russians. There were *extras*. Intourist did not exactly specify what the extras were. They were simply extras. The upshot was that he paid twenty-one dollars on top of the eight days' rental he had already been conned into paying in advance.

"To add insult to injury," he said, "When I started to pay the extra charges in rubles, the young man shook his head emphatically. Intourist was interested only in Western currency." Yergin concluded plaintively, "I sometimes got the feeling that Western currency was Intourist's only real interest in me."

I was witness to the mind-blowing flagrancy with which the gallused and bobby-pinned Canadians were taken. The Russians almost made a joke of it. Now Moscow is to be the host to the Olympics in 1980, and this book has been attempted as both a guide to the reader—what to expect and what not to expect—and how to enjoy himself by rising above it all. Moscow can be fun, and Moscow *is* fun, but it is hell for anyone who asks more than it is prepared to deliver.

There is not the slightest evidence that the authorities have any intention of improving hotel and restaurant service. Already worse than it was in Joseph Stalin's time, it will get even more atrocious as the rapaciousness for tips gets stronger, and the prospect of booty grows brighter. The official Soviet caterers have more important things to think about than coping with the caprices of complaining tourists. They are thinking about

Money—an unimaginable cornucopia of dollars, marks, yen, Arab gold, even pounds sterling.

The advice of this very seasoned traveler to Moscow, hard-bitten, occasionally frostbitten, and withal affectionate, is this: from the moment you arrive until the moment you leave, *do not tip a single kopek to anybody for anything.* Argue about everything. Do not take no for an answer. Simulate bad temper even if you are in perfectly good humor, because bad temper, alas, is the Soviet way of life.

If the maître d'hôtel, sitting smoking in a corner and working out his receipts when you come in for lunch, says there is no table in a half-empty restaurant. There is no point in simply sitting down at an empty table, because no one will take any notice of you. Hover over him and drive him out of his mind. Make him think you are going to sit in his lap. Hiss *"Stol"* (table) into his ear at the precise moment he is about to complete his addition, so that he has to start all over again. You will get a seat, probably at a table for four, with three strangers. But at least you will be fed sooner or later.

And then, after you have had your meal (borscht and chicken Kiev are always the most reliable orders, though you can't live on the two forever), if you return to your room and find the beds unmade and the room uncleaned, don't call the housekeeper, because nobody will come. Throw the sheets and bathroom towels into the corridor.

They'll understand.

14

The Necktie from GUM

By any standard Gorky Street is one of the great avenues of the world. It combines tsarist sweep and Stalin *Schadenfreude*. It is strange how a certain quaint, horror-movie charm has accumulated around Stalin's architectural heritage: the wedding-cake skyscrapers and even Karl Marx Allee in East Berlin, which I still think of fondly as Stalin Allee.

Most of what Moscow has to offer can be found along Gorky Street. Historically it was part of the trading road to Tver (now Kalinin) on the Volga. As Tver Street it became the city's principal thoroughfare at the beginning of the eighteenth century; an interesting parallel with New York's Broadway, which began life as the Boston Post Road.

The name was changed from Tver to Gorky in 1932. In 1937 Stalin ordered reconstruction work to widen even further the broad avenue. When I first went to Moscow there was no street neon display at all, and a night stroll along Gorky Street had all the cultural stimulation of a similar stroll through, say, Wilkes-Barre, Pennsylvania. Today it blazes with light like Piccadilly. Advertisements flash on and off, dominating the upper stories of the great buildings. There is a caveat: only official government interests, like Aeroflot, can be advertised. Western concerns are not completely banned from display. A company like, say, ITT, can display itself, but only in the Western compounds. It can say only "ITT" and may not be illuminated by more than a single electric light bulb!

After a horrified look at the dreadful Central Telegraph Office, the street's most famous monument to Stalin's taste, one can cross the avenue by underpass and have a sundae or a "flying saucer" at the Cosmos Café. You will taste some of the world's best ice cream, if the waiting line is not unendurably long. Along the street are innumerable stand-up snack bars where edible buns and undrinkable coffee are served. If you ask for "coffee with milk," be warned that the milk is probably condensed.

Farther along Gorky Street, on the right going up, stands one of the greatest food shops in the entire world. Not for what one gets, but for what one sees. No building in Moscow evokes more clearly how the well-to-do lived in tsarist times. Today it is simply called Gastronom 1, but it is the famous Eliseyev Grocery Store. Gilt, ceramic decorations and enormous cascading chandeliers overwhelm the senses. Before the First World War, it was to Moscow what Fortnum and Mason is to London. New York has no equivalent. It is even more glorious than the Metro, more spectacular than any other food store on earth.

What it serves doesn't matter. Just to enter is to move into history, to become aware of life as it was and is no longer. Pushing through the lines of shoddily clad, ill-mannered people, from mountains of cabbage to mountains of turnips, past counters with bottles of sticky-looking syrups in green, red and blue, past sausages and more sausages, one should see the past not the sordid present. The store should be, and once was, filled with all the delicacies of Europe and Asia. It is a place of sheer enchantment. The only thing worth buying there, if one is prepared to queue for an hour or so, is cheese.

The other way to acquire the feel of old Moscow is to visit the remaining private mansions and those kitchens Gastronom 1 used so sumptuously to serve. Some are open to the public, although for others one must apply for a special permit. The latter, being less trodden, are the most interesting.

One requiring permission is the Yusupov House on the Ulitsa Bolshovo Karitonevskovo. It is the small, exquisite palace of the Yusupov family, now the home of the Academy of Agricultural Science. It was built at the end of the seventeenth century on the site of a hunting lodge belonging to Ivan the Terrible. It is astounding to learn, seeing it now in the middle of Moscow, that Yusupov built around it a garden which in its time was compared to Versailles. Pushkin as a boy played in it. The garden was burned in 1812, during Napoleon's occupation.

Prince Yusupov, he who murdered Rasputin in 1917, told me in Paris some years before his death that he had been invited by the Soviet Ministry of Fine Arts to return as curator to his Moscow and Leningrad homes. His reply was, "Yuk! Among all those smelly Bolshies! The only reason I killed Rasputin was because he smelled so bad."

The Romanov House and connecting Znamensky Monastery is, I believe, open to the public. It was the birthplace of the Tsar Michael, the first Romanov to sit on the Russian throne. It is the typical house of a rich boyar, with cellars for cold storage and on the second floor a kitchen which for magnificence rivals the kitchen of the Royal Pavilion in Brighton, England.

Above the house one can still see the Romanov coat of arms—a winged griffin clutching a sword and shield. Most of the valuable possessions have disappeared, and the sixteenth-century monastery built behind the house is in pathetic condition. The address is 18 Ulitsa Razina—you can't miss it, because the Hotel Rossiya stands in what used to be its grounds.

A fabulous and very accessible nineteenth-century house is the *Dom Druzhba* (the House of Friendship with the Peoples of Foreign Countries) at number 16 Kalinin Prospect. Even in New York there are mansions older than this, built by similar kinds of millionaires for similar reasons of prestige. It was erected by a merchant called Morozov and combines Moorish and Spanish architecture. Rather too many friendly peoples of foreign countries have trampled its floors since it was opened as the *Dom*

Druzhba in 1959, and the battered feeling is accentuated by the propaganda photographs and Xeroxed bulletins on the walls. But one can enter, look around at the staircases and frescoes and feel, vividly, how it originally *was*.

Some of the homes of the nineteenth-century writers and musicians are open to visitors. One of the most interesting is the Tolstoy home at 21 Ulitsa Lyova Tolstova. The house has been faithfully preserved as Tolstoy and his family lived in it, and one gets a good feeling of his mode of living. Chekhov's home is at 6 Sadovaya Kudrinskaya. There's not much of Chekhov left there, but it is still worth a visit.

Most of the other residences of the eighteenth- and nineteenth-century quality are now government offices, dreadfully neglected inside.

The mansions that have been turned into offices cannot be entered, but they are well worth studying from the outside by architecture buffs. My favorite is the Ryabushinsky House at number 2 Ulitsa Kachalova, with its startling, early-twentieth-century Art Nouveau façade.

Despite the above excursions around Moscow, my readers will have accepted that this is not a travel book but merely the impressions of Moscow by a regular, affectionate and exasperated visitor. The same readers, however, may appreciate a few general and useful hints on how to get along in this most baffling of cities. The suggestions are offered in no particular order.

For your wardrobe, select your oldest clothes: you will still look smart by Moscow standards. To explain why you should take your oldest clothes, I shall appear to digress. In spite of all these descriptions of Moscow indifference, you are still likely to make friends through happenstance. In the restaurants one is almost invariably seated among strangers. Here Moscow indifference evaporates, and you will soon be smattering your few words together and trying to communicate. Take this conversation from one visit of mine:

I was sitting alone in the restaurant of the Berlin Hotel. A young couple asked if the other places at the table were taken. I uttered a polite *"Pazholuista"* and they sat down and stared at me curiously. Very diffidently the young man touched my arm and said *"Anglisky?"* I acknowledged it, more or less, and the two young people smiled. There was a long pause, and the young man spoke up again, in English:

"Nineteen to nine."

"Dynamo," I replied.

"Matthews," he said.

"Fomitch," I countered.

We all three shook hands and ordered vodka for mutual toasts. We knew exactly what we were talking about even though that was more or less the limit of their English, and from then on we smattered along in German. In 1945, as part of the victory celebrations, the Soviet Union sent a soccer team, the Moscow Dynamos, to Britain. They played four games: won two, tied two, scored nineteen goals, gave up nine. Stanley Matthews, England's right-winger, is to soccer history what Babe Ruth is to baseball, even down to the spindly legs, and "Tiger" Fomitch was the Dynamos' goalkeeper.

The Russians on that occasion behaved with the appalling rudeness that has since become familiar to us all; tempers frayed on the field and at the subsequent banquets. The Russians cut their visit short, went home in filthy tempers and declared the whole thing a Soviet triumph against Fascism, proving the superiority of Soviet manhood.

In fact, Russian soccer players were not drafted into the war because they were considered too important for Russian morale, while most of the British players left their khakhi uniforms in the locker rooms to go out to play. Also, the massive difference in goals was distorted by a 10–1 victory over a Welsh minor league team; the other results were 3–3, 4–3, 2–2. The Russians then produced a stage musical about it called *Nineteen to Nine*, in which one of the English managers was portrayed as a notorious

Fascist caught trying to slip a Mickey into the tea of the noble Russian players.

How is this relevant to old clothes? Because such is how friendships are made in Moscow. After a few more meetings with the young couple I was happy to offer him a suit, and he more than delighted to take it. A suit you were thinking of throwing away becomes a gesture of good will and friendship.

The traveler should also take along several lipsticks to brighten the smiles of the friends he has made or for the occasionally cheerful Berioska girl. Take also Wilkinson razor blades. It is important that they should be Wilkinson, because one can then remind the recipient that it was that firm which forged the sword which King George VI presented to Stalin after the Battle of Stalingrad, now called the Battle of the Volga. The double allusion, to British royalty and to Stalin will embarrass them or make them scowl, but one is entitled to a little fun at their expense.

Take chocolate bars and highly scented soaps in elegant wrapping. Take a few copies of *Vogue, Elle,* and *Paris-Match* for those more interested in world events but whose command of foreign languages is limited. I suspect they wouldn't dig *Cosmopolitan.* The girlie magazines could get you into trouble—a bitch-minded chambermaid could decide to complain.

On more general terms: before you leave for Moscow, make sure your hanger tabs are attached to your overcoats. Theater cloakroom attendants get very nasty if you don't have the tabs, and sling the coats over the hook to ensure that you have a bulge on your shoulder when you put your coat on afterward.

As the checking of overcoats, bags, etc. is obligatory everywhere, there are always huge queues waiting after a theater performance. Here is a reliable tip for legitimate queue jumping. Before the performance, rent binoculars—they cost only a few kopeks. The queue waiting to return them is always much shorter than the other, and the old lady with the babushka, as she takes your binoculars, will also get your coat.

Carry two kopeks for making calls in pay telephones. In order to call you must put the coin in *before* you pick up the receiver. Why do Russians do *everything* the other way around?

Russians change their schedules arbitrarily, for all sorts of reasons or sometimes no reason at all. Museums may be closed without notice—for inventory, inspections, renovations, purges of the curators (they don't say that). Worse, theater and movie schedules will also be changed. *The Cherry Orchard* might be listed as playing at the Moscow Art Theater. You want to see it because you know it and can laugh and cry in the right places. You buy your ticket from Intourist and proceed to the theater, a modern, architecturally exciting building on the Khudoztrenny Proyezd, just off Gorky Street.

Although no announcement is made, you find yourself watching something from Gogol you do not understand at all. Don't complain to Intourist next day. They could not care less and will give you the famous Moscow shrug.

Don't expect that just because you are you, and all Moscow tourism is supposed to be geared for you, that you will automatically be given tickets for any theater performance you want to see. The lady at Intourist may tell you that there are no more tickets for the Bolshoi or Moyseyev for the entire period of your stay. This happened to me once, on the first day of my arrival, and with three weeks to go—the effect was shattering. But I tried the next hotel and was issued all the tickets I wanted. The Intourist lady in question may just have had a quarrel with another incensed tourist and was compensating by hating everybody.

Experienced stamp collectors will spot immediately that the packets of precanceled Soviet stamps at all Moscow hotel newsstands are nothing more than a government-operated fraud against tourists. In any philately store in the United States, even the expensive Gimbels, similar packets can be bought for half the price. But nonexperts seeking souvenirs for their children or friends at home may well be tricked into buying a packet. Don't.

On the other hand, the buying of current stamps from the

mail departments of the hotels is usually a pleasure, and the Russians issue a stamp for every bird that falls. For some reason—another Moscow insoluble—the young ladies behind the counters of the mail sections are always the friendliest of Muscovites to deal with. This tradition continues for year after year, and provides relief from the snarls and shrugs one receives everywhere else. They will often hand over their entire portfolio of stamps for the collector to browse through at his leisure.

The girls are cheery and actually identify with their customers. After a visitor has checked in with them day after day inquiring for mail, they will hail him as he enters the door, "A letter for you at last! It's from Melbourne."

Similar friendliness can be found from the ladies behind the counter of the Central Telegraph Office. I was once even given a farewell present by one of the telegraphists there. It was only a little booklet of colored views of Moscow, but it was a very touching gesture. I suppose it springs from the stimulation of handling letters and telegrams from faraway places with strange-sounding names. Vicariously, through their customers, they are world travelers.

At the hotel newsstands only Communist publications can be bought officially—an outrageous anachronism in a major tourist city and another slap in the face for people bringing millions of dollars into the country's exchequer. The Helsinki Agreement of 1974 hasn't changed a thing. If you want to read the news, you have to read it in the London *Morning Star*, which is almost unreadable. Or, if you read French, you can buy the far superior *Humanité*.

However, the lady behind the counter usually has copies of the International *Herald Tribune* and the Fleet Street newspapers which she keeps *under the counter* like dirty books, which indeed she probably considers them to be. *Pravda*, as everyone well knows, should be good enough for anybody who wants all the news that's fit to print. She is usually among the nastier of the people tourists encounter. She is the mails lady and the telegraph lady in reverse, because she is dealing in obscene merchandise. If there are a lot of people crowding around for postcards and souvenirs, she is likely to deny any knowledge of such newspapers. But if business is quiet she will pull out a copy between finger and thumb and accept the money silently, with pursed lips and averted head.

Because of phony rates of exchange, prices in GUM on Red Square and in the rather better-class TsUM on the Petrovka behind the Bolshoi Theater are higher than those of Saks Fifth Avenue or Harrods. (The official rate is seventy-five cents to the ruble. On the free markets of the West, a dollar buys no fewer than six rubles.)

The famous Detsky Mir (Children's World) is always primly pointed out by guides as an example and symbol of the peace-loving intentions of the Soviet Union. The shop sells no toy soldiers, no cannons, no model battleships, no toys of war at all. What it does sell is a load of shoddy rubbish. Children in wartime Britain were better fitted out and played with better-quality toys.

But shopping in the department stores, even when buffeted by hordes of unsweet Muscovites, can still be a lot of fun. In tsarist times the huge GUM building was a market, consisting of row after row and gallery upon gallery of small privately owned *soukhs*. The *soukh* principle continues today. Unlike TsUM or Detsky Mir, it is not a department store in the Western sense of the word, but a series of small- and medium-size self-contained shops. Some of the souvenir shops have almost a touch of class among them, and others can almost be called boutiques. There are pharmacies and candy stores. Larger shops sell clothes and shoes. Tiny bars dispense champagne. There one can stand around sipping and keep an eye open for where the action is. One can always tell by the pell-mell rush which follows delivery of each new consignment.

Whatever bargain is being offered, buy it on the spot, and push the competition to the ground before it pushes you. Clutch your purchase carefully to your bosom (because it will be wrapped carelessly in a bit of paper that would rip on the cutting edge of a tea bag), and struggle away to avoid suffocation. Don't even seek to try it on. The Muscovite practice is to buy it, try it on later and, if it doesn't fit, swap it with a friend for something else.

It was while consuming an ice cream in one of GUM's multiple-storied alleyways that I saw the consignment of ties arrive at a boutique in cartons borne by an old lady in a babushka.

The Russians, traditionally tieless, or at best a one-tie-per-person-per-lifetime society, have become very tie-conscious in the last few years. Recently, at a store called the Tie Haberdashery on Stoleshnikov Lane in downtown Moscow, a kind of electronic poll was conducted to find out Russian taste in ties. A display was held of nearly one hundred sample neckties. People were allowed to examine and feel for quality, then press a button registering the number of the tie they liked best. According to the announcement, the most popular style would go into production in due course. The vote went according to width, cloth, preference for stripes, dots, foulards.

The spectacle was watched by Christopher Wren of *The New York Times*, who found that the single most popular tie was number 51, a butterscotch item with one broad, diagonal brown stripe. Generally the Muscovites avoided excessively bright and excessively wide ties and preferred conservative colors of gray, dark blue and maroon.

Wren heard one customer ask, "When can I buy one of these?"

The display organizer thought the question over and said, "Probably by the end of May."

"You mean another year and a half," the customer replied. Those around him laughed understandingly, and the organizer did not argue.

But there, in front of my eyes, in GUM, I saw the neckties

arriving. Many were very pleasing by any standards, with prices ranging from two dollars to five dollars, and I, with my ice cream still only half consumed, found myself closest to the consignment and first in line. For four dollars I selected a handsome, conservative tie in a black and red sheeny foulard. It would have won a seal of approval for neatness and good taste back on Madison Avenue from the brothers Brooks.

I would have bought more, but by the time I had paid for the one they were all sold out. In less than five minutes only a few stringy lengths of colored cloth were left on the racks.

A week or so later I returned to London and attended a cocktail party in Cadogan Gardens, Chelsea, held to celebrate an I.R.A. bomb which had gone off across the road the night before without injuring anybody. Standing in remaining bits of broken glass I found myself talking to John Cavanagh, one of London's top fashion designers, a specialist in men's fashion who has left his own distinctive taste on necktie design. I opened my mouth to say, "Hey, guess where I got—"

I was given no chance to finish my sentence. Cavanagh said, "I like your tie. Where did you buy it?"

John Cavanagh liked my tie! This surely was the kind of feed line that can come but once in a lifetime. It is rather like Dame Margot Fonteyn at a ball saying, "You dance divinely." Excitedly I answered, "Believe it or not, I bought it in GUM in Moscow only last week. Off the rack, just like that. None of your Berioska hard-currency stuff. Berioska shopping is for tourists. This was the real thing . . . I was standing there . . . eating an ice cream, minding my own business, then up comes this old babushka carting about six kilos of ties on her back, so I rushed in . . . and . . . and . . ."

I saw too late that I had overplayed my hand, or at least had overexposed my tie. There are certain place names that turn on certain people, and certain place names that don't. I happen to be finishing this book here and now, in Lisbon. Portugal is in the middle of a revolution, guns are firing and the windows are closed to keep out the tear gas. Yet when I telephone London, or New York, or Paris, everyone says, "You are in Lisbon? How lovely! Lucky *you!* What's the weather like?"

John Cavanagh, I realized, did not include Moscow as one of the places that turned him on, and I had exhausted his interest in my necktie and the sociological significance of shopping in GUM. "Really?" he said politely, and by mutual consent we changed the subject.

That is not quite the end of the story. After about three weeks and four more knottings of my GUM tie—making six formal appearances in all—something began to happen to it. The inner lining began to warp and twist, and at the bottom of the tie the stitching began to go slack like catgut. No matter how meticulously I tied the knot, or how lovingly I smoothed it down the front, the tie assumed the shape of a boomerang. It had to go.

And I guess *that* is the end of the story.

But, Moscow, I love you anyway. In your shabby, dotty, horrible, repulsive, lovable way, you are bigger than both of us.